Logan Pearsall Smith

**The youth of Parnassus and other stories**

Logan Pearsall Smith

**The youth of Parnassus and other stories**

ISBN/EAN: 9783744748759

Printed in Europe, USA, Canada, Australia, Japan

Cover: Foto ©Andreas Hilbeck / pixelio.de

More available books at **www.hansebooks.com**

# The Youth of Parnassus

and Other Stories

by
Logan Pearsall Smith

London
Macmillan and Co.
and New York
1895

*All rights reserved*

To
Philip Morrell

# Contents

|  | Page |
|---|---|
| The Youth of Parnassus | 1 |
| The Will to Live. I. | 79 |
| The Will to Live. II. | 99 |
| The Claim of the Past | 125 |
| A Broken Journey | 143 |
| The Sub-Warden | 183 |
| Idyll | 201 |
| Buller Intervening | 243 |
| The Optimist | 259 |

*The Youth of Parnassus*

A

# The Youth of Parnassus

I.

HE came straight to Oxford from his American home, Parnassus City, a town in the Western State of Indiana.

The first time Foley saw him was one wet October evening, when, splashing across the quadrangle towards his rooms, he noticed a large umbrella moving through the dripping twilight—an umbrella which, from its undecided motion, must belong, he had told himself, to some tourist, who, in spite of the rain and darkness, was finishing a day of sight-seeing at

St. Mary's. But when the umbrella collapsed in front of his own staircase, and Foley saw the spectacles and pale face of a young man who turned to enter there, he decided that it must be an agent, come to collect money for missions or something of the kind. And as he followed upstairs, in the wet footprints of the feet he could still hear mounting above him, he asked himself with vague annoyance what right they had—people like that—to push themselves into the rooms of Oxford men.

The melancholy footsteps went on till they reached the top; nor did Foley hear them again descend. Soon after he was told that an American had come into College, and was living above him; and when he went to call, he recognized, in the person who awkwardly rose to receive him, the young man he had taken for a mission agent in the rain that evening. A thin, small young man, in a long, black broadcloth coat of provincial cut, he seemed at first sight nothing but the traditional Western American Foley had read of in books, or seen in the theatre sometimes—a student who looked curiously out of place in that old panelled room

The young Englishman talked to him as best he could, asking the questions always asked of a new-comer; questions which this one answered with the usual shyness, but in a very unusual voice and accent.

He had just come from America; he had left there on the sixth. He had come to study under Dr. Joseph at the new Methodist College. Dr. Joseph had arranged for him to come to St. Mary's; their own College wasn't built yet. Foley asked if he thought he would like Oxford. "Yes, sir," the other replied, drawing a large handkerchief from his coat-tails, "I guess I will; though," he added cautiously after a moment, "it does seem kind of old and mouldy."

Foley thought he had done his duty in calling, and meant for the future to see as little as possible of his new neighbour. And yet there had been something pleasant and sensitive in his face, he remembered afterwards; and at times he was haunted by the thought of this stranger sitting as he had found him, alone and lonely in the room upstairs, with two or three books in the empty shelves, a few photographs of home that made the mantelpiece and bare walls look all the more homeless and unfriendly. Now and then he would hear footsteps above moving vaguely about, or he would meet the American on the stairs, or see him walking out alone, and at last, out of kindness, he went again to call.

Before long he began to take a certain

liking to Sutton, and would often go up in the evenings with a cigarette to his rooms. To the young Englishman the American was certainly a curious and amusing study. How curious were the views and impressions of Oxford, that, breaking through his shy reserve, he would once in a while express, in his prim middle-aged way! He was a good deal shocked by the wine-drinking, card-playing, and Sabbath-breaking that seemed so prevalent there; what religion there was, (well, he didn't guess there was much,) he thought mechanical and dead. Of course there was a great deal of culture in Oxford; but in other things, like telephones and electric lights, why England was behind the Mississippi Valley!

## II.

Foley began to have ideas of his own about this Mississippi Valley. He had already read of its rivers and railways and mushroom towns, and he remembered some of the proud things that Sutton had said at different times of Parnassus City and its importance—it was almost the only subject on which the reticent young man ever seemed willing to talk—the thought-out comparisons he would draw between that place and Oxford, in his attempts to explain to himself what he saw, and account for it all, according to his principles.

One evening, in a burst of unusual talkativeness, he described how Parnassus City had been laid out twenty years before, on what had been till then an unploughed prairie; but now there were thousands of inhabitants, rows of business buildings, and elegant residences in the outskirts. There were electric trolleys too in the streets; and the whole town was lighted by natural gas. Not only had the place grown fast in trade and population, but there had been, he explained, a pretty rapid growth in culture. Oh, they didn't intend to let the moss grow on them out in Indiana! Schools and churches were built—the most elegant was the First Methodist, the Reverend Dr. Turnpenny's. It was Dr. Turnpenny, he added, who started the Forward Movement among the Indiana Methodists which made such a stir. Then, after the churches, they had built a lecture hall and library, and, at last, the Parnassus College.

Foley asking more about this college, Sutton explained that though it had been built a few years before as a college for Methodist theology and liberal learning, it was already larger than the neighbouring institute at Corinth

Creek, and only second in those parts to the University of Miomi. It wasn't of course like the universities in the Eastern States, but still they were proud of it there.

He had pinned up on the old panelling of his wall a photograph of this Parnassus College: a rather gaunt frame building, standing in a ploughed field among a few new-planted trees. About the steps were grouped a number of young men and women, many of them wearing spectacles, and all with earnest faces and provincial dress. "That's my class," Sutton explained, pointing at his own figure in the group. "It's the biggest class we've had so far, thirteen gentlemen and seven ladies."

Foley studied the photograph of the college, and the pictures on the mantelpiece—several college friends, with lank serious faces; an intellectual young lady, her hand resting on a copy of the Bible; and an old, mild, white bearded minister—Dr. Turnpenny, no doubt. There was a picture too of a wide city street. Then it really existed, this remote place, and people lived there! he thought, amused at the curious chance which had brought Sutton, the promise and pride, perhaps, of his native town, and set him down in so different a world.

But at last Foley turned from the yellow lamplight, the photographs, and the voice of the American sawing in his ear. Going to the window he opened the lattice and leaned out into the night. Cool, fresh, and dark was the air that breathed on his face, while before him, blue and vague under the white moon, there grew on his sight the towers, the dome-like trees, and shining roofs of Oxford; dim, romantic, and steeped in silence, save for the even tinkle of a distant bell. With sudden unaffected sentiment, he felt how much he cared for Oxford and all that Oxford stood for.

"Do come here," he called out with a friendly impulse, turning his head into the yellow light of the room, "I don't think I ever saw such a view."

The American came and leaned beside him at the open window. "Yes, it is nice," he said at length, and Foley was surprised by a fugitive sound of real feeling and appreciation in his voice.

### III.

Gradually he came to take a more real interest in his neighbour. The books that Sutton read, Sutton's love of poetry—surprised him; little things he would say now and then seemed to show indications of sensitive fancies and shy feelings hardly in accordance with his dry exterior. What a thing it would be for him, Foley thought, if the poor young man's taste could be really cultivated; if he could only be set free from his narrowing ideas and made to look at life for himself, instead of seeing it always through the grey fog of Puritan prejudice!

Sutton took everything that Foley said with delightful seriousness; the well-worn arguments against Democracy and Republicanism were new to him, and seemed to puzzle him—he would come days afterwards with carefully thought-out answers to them. Or he would give his friend tracts to read, as if he was worried by Foley's ritualistic tastes, and hoped to convert him to Methodism; and once he persuaded him to go and hear Dr. Joseph preach. Foley was really impressed by the good sense and vigour of Sutton's master, but to Sutton himself he criticized what he thought a want of beauty in the service.

And it was only once that Foley felt even

for a moment the least uncomfortable about the things he said to his friend—one evening when he happened to run upstairs with some specious argument about the Apostolic Succession, (for when an idea occurred to him he liked to make use of it at once,) and going into the American's room, he found him on his knees in prayer.

In that old place—for St. Mary's was not one of the more liberal Colleges, but a sleepy, ancient, aristocratic society, very conservative of its own beliefs and manners and prejudices —Eliaphet Sutton lived on at first, unknown to almost everybody, and only noticed for the oddness of his looks, as he went in and out to his lectures or solitary walks. But after a while Foley's interest in him, and his own shy charm of manner, gained him a more friendly welcome in the College, and little by little he began to modify, it was remarked, the quaint unconventionalities of his speech and ways.

A curious life it was, this Oxford life into which the inexperienced American had chanced to drift! A community of young men, generously bred and taught, living together so intimately in that mediaeval place, with its own old usages and traditions and ways of thinking; shut out, as by a high wall, from the world outside; aloof from the vulgar needs of life; concerned, many of them, only with its theoretic problems, interested more, perhaps, in the ancient Greeks than in contemporary affairs—and, indeed, not unlike the Greeks in their care for the clearness and beauty of the mind, the athletic strength of the body—surely, Foley thought, the young Methodist could not have found so delightful a place in all the world beside.

How much he was really influenced by it

Foley could not tell; certainly as the months went by he seemed to be more aware of the beauty of Oxford; he would stop sometimes of his own accord to look through a blue gateway or down a sunlit street, and once Foley saw him standing, a quaint figure, under the University Church, and gazing up at the spire—at the religious statues there, which seemed to be voyaging through the windy sky and among its great white clouds. He started to join him, but Sutton, seeing he was noticed, moved hastily away.

Then Foley remembered an evening when, coming out into the quadrangle, he saw a figure he recognized as Sutton's standing at a barred gate opening on the street. In front of the American, through that one small opening in the great dark walls, was the gas-lit yellow of the street, the noise of the passing crowd and traffic—for it was the evening of a market day—but at his back the deep shadow and silence of the old quadrangle.

"It's rather absurd to be locked up in this way," Foley said, joining him; but Sutton replied after a moment, "Why, I was just thinking I rather liked it! Of course it is absurd, but still—" He stopped, as he so often stopped, in the middle of his sentence.

Other times there were when Sutton seemed curiously narrow and stubborn; times when some of his dissenting acquaintances had just been to see him—the elderly undergraduates, with bald heads and big moustaches, whom Foley took to be pupils of Dr. Joseph's when he met them mounting the stairs. One of these dissenting friends of the American's, a friendly, awkward young man, named Abel, who was assistant tutor to Dr. Joseph, and had come with him to Oxford when the college moved there from Birmingham, seemed to have a special supervision over the American. Abel had no very high idea of Oxford and Oxford people, and once, when they met in Sutton's rooms, he and Foley argued a little about the University.

Anyhow he envied Sutton, Abel said at last, turning, as he rose to go, to the silent American; it wasn't everybody who had the luck to live in such a place. But Sutton suddenly coloured, and answered, "You can't blame me, Abel, Dr. Turnpenny wanted me...."

"I'm not blaming you, my friend, it's only envy," Abel replied good-humouredly. He still lingered a moment, looking at the books, and cross-questioning Sutton about his work, and how he spent his time.

Foley, who liked anything new, was interested by this intelligent, tactless man, and wondered why Sutton should be so obviously glad when at last the young dissenter went his way.

## IV

The next day Foley found his friend in a mood of deep depression. He would not go out anywhere, he said; he must spend the afternoon—indeed, he meant to spend all his afternoons now—on his work; he had been neglecting it too long. And though this desperate resolve was often broken, yet from this time on he seemed subject now and then to moods of troubled conscience—moods in which he would shut himself up, sometimes for days, working feverishly alone, or only coming to his friend late at night to talk in an uneasy, interrupted way about the sinfulness of the world, and its pleasures, and how wrong it was to enjoy yourself. At these notions Foley would laugh, or argue seriously against them. That Sutton could have any real reason for feeling as he did, Foley never suspected, but thought it simply the old moroseness which haunted him, the unreasoned hatred of the Puritans for gaiety and life. And Sutton had very little to say in answer to his friend. Yes, he was getting on with his work well enough, he admitted, and there was nothing really to keep him from going out, except—except—somehow he felt it was wrong.

But the wrong thing, Foley declared, was to stay in-doors all those beautiful summer days; and then more seriously he added, that he was sure what Sutton needed was to see more of the world and life. Living in his lonely retired way, what could he know of other people and the things they cared for, and how could he ever hope to have any influence on them? And, once convinced that it was his duty, Sutton became curiously eager to shut up his books and go.

# The Youth of Parnassus

Indeed, for the most part, the poor young man was not hard to influence, Foley found; any strong assertion attracted him, and he was often only too willing to resign to someone else the responsibility of deciding what he ought to do. But then again he would grow suddenly so stubborn and prejudiced; and at all times he was so reserved about himself and his own feelings, that the young Englishman, in spite of his theories, never felt he really understood him. Perhaps, he sometimes fancied, Sutton had no very real ideas or impressions of his own; perhaps he was not influenced by Oxford in the least, and was not aware of any real difference between the ancient town, with its traditions and memories, and the new-built Parnassus City

## V.

But when Foley had left Oxford and gone abroad that summer, the long letters that came to him now and then, written in Sutton's fine clerklike hand, surprised and touched him a little. It was odd, he thought, that a person who had talked with so much reserve, should write him such charming and intimate letters, and he told himself he had always believed there were real feelings and tastes behind Sutton's mask of awkward silence.

The first of the letters was written in the vacation just after Foley had gone abroad. It was Sutton's first summer in Europe; he was staying on at Oxford, having friends nowhere else, and not being able, of course, to go back to America. But from the way he wrote, America was plainly a good deal in his thoughts, and often in those long still days he wished himself back there, haunted as he was by the idea that he might be wasting his time, that what he was learning in Oxford might not be of any use to him out in Indiana after all. But then he really knew, he wrote, that he was doing the best thing in staying on. The church out there, and indeed the whole country, was growing so rapidly, that there would be need in the ministry for young men who were well trained, and familiar with the thought and culture of the day. He had come to see that Foley was right in saying it was your duty to get familiar with modern ideas, and read modern books; he was getting on with the list of books Foley had made for him. Of course you ought to understand, or at least try to understand, your opponent's views. If you were afraid of this, it showed, as Dr. Turnpenny always said, that you could not be very sure of yourself.

Indeed, when Dr. Turnpenny had advised him to come to Oxford, he had felt it would prove to the world that, at any rate the Indiana Methodists were quite assured of their position.

In the next letter there was a mention of the American tourists who were coming through the summer in such numbers to Oxford. Sutton used to watch them when they walked into the quiet College garden, where he sat alone, wishing he knew them and could talk to them about America. Their voices and ways made them seem like old friends to him there in that strange country. Once two ladies had asked him the way to the chapel, and he had been delighted to show them the sights of the College. They were from Buffalo, New York; he must be sure to call on them, they said, if he ever came to Buffalo. They told him how much they would like to stay on in Oxford—but they had to go back to America in a month. Sutton envied them their quick return; but after all, he added, when the time came, probably he might be a little sorry to leave Oxford. . . .


## VI.

Then in the autumn, Sutton wrote about the coming together of the College, the beginning of busy life after the long quiet of the vacation days. For the first time he had gone to service in the College chapel. He did not like the way of worship, finding it formal and meaningless; but gradually, as the twilight faded away, and the great painted windows filled with darkness—growing black in the candle-lit walls about them—another impression came to him, looking at all those faces in the dim light, and listening to their voices —an impression of the unity and living spirit of the College, as being a small, ancient commonwealth, with a history and traditions of its own. There they all were, just themselves, shut in from the world outside, gathered together, as the College had gathered together in the same place for five or six hundred years. Though he was only there as a spectator, who had chanced to wander in from the outside, yet he realized how great an influence such a place, with all its old ways and customs, might have on the young Englishmen who came there. Indeed, if the influence had not been so obviously narrow and deadening he himself might have been a little affected by it. . . .

"Yes, you were right," he said in another letter, "when you told me that the antiquity of England belongs to us Americans as much as to you. . . . Sometimes I fancy I had an ancestor here once; I am sure he was a Puritan, and disapproved of the ecclesiasticism and worldliness of the place. And yet, poor man, he could not help loving Oxford too. A retired, melancholy person, he liked it best in the days like these when the buildings and yellow and greenish trees are half veiled in the autumn mist. But at last he went over with the Puritans to New England, and was much better and more active there, and free from all the dreamy influences that held him in Oxford. And it will be much better for me too, when I go back next year."

### VII.

But he had almost decided to go back at once, he wrote in the next letter. He saw now, and indeed all along he had felt deep down in his soul, that he was doing wrong in staying there; that there was nothing really in Oxford to help him. If Foley only knew all the circumstances he would understand. And, in any case, it was not wholesome to be always living in the past.

And in Oxford you *were* in the past; the dead were about you everywhere; you dwelt in the buildings they had built, you read their books, you thought their thoughts, and the weight of their dreary traditions crushed down on you, forcing your life into the shape of theirs. Surely there was something evil and haunted about the place! And during all those dripping autumn days, Sutton's one thought had been a longing to be back again under the keen skies of his prairie-home; life was new and hopeful there, unshadowed by the gloom of antiquity and death. . . .

But soon after Sutton wrote that he had had a talk with Dr. Joseph. "He advises me by all means to stay here. He says that all I am getting at Oxford will certainly be very useful to me when I go back. I never had an idea how strong our position is; I wish you might have a talk with him sometime, when you return. He explains that religion is progressive; that there is no real antagonism between the new and the old; the one has grown out of the other by a natural evolution. Indeed he laughed at the idea of being afraid of the Past; one ought to enjoy it, not fear it, he said. Then when I asked him if there wasn't a danger in the new criticism, and too much reasoning about things, he said that there never could be any real danger in following one's best reason, and that we need not be the least afraid of what it will lead us to."

## VIII.

Other letters came to Foley now and then. Sutton spoke of his work and occupations, the taciturn young man taking a certain pleasure, as it seemed, in writing down the ideas and impressions that he found it hard to express in any other way.

But Foley at this time was travelling in the East; he could only read the American's letters with haste and small attention. Some, however, he put aside to keep, and now and then would write back in a disconnected way, for he felt a certain friendliness for this assiduous correspondent. As time went on, however, the letters grew more infrequent, and at last the correspondence died. Foley, with his new interests, had almost forgotten Sutton, or would only think of him vaguely as a preacher somewhere in America, whither doubtless he had returned some time ago.

## IX.

After Foley had spent a year or two almost entirely abroad, he returned to England, began working hard at his profession, and it was some time before he found the leisure to go back to Oxford. At last he went one midsummer alone, for an idle visit. It was the vacation; the old College was almost deserted, and sometimes in the evening he would go into the garden there, and, sitting under one of the great trees, would read, or idly watch the fading of the twilight. And now memories of the old days, and sentiments towards a place which he had once loved with a certain enthusiasm—though half forgetting it afterwards, amid his other occupations—came back to him with unexpected vividness. How much more delightful it made life, he told himself one evening, as he sat there, half lost in sentimental musing, how much more delightful it made life to have been at Oxford, to have learned to love the place as one did learn to love it—to have it always as a charming memory! It was so perfect, that evening, with the sunset still lingering faint and red behind the blue trees and towers, up there above the dusky garden stretches. And that figure of a cloistered student which Foley could vaguely distinguish on the twilight path; it was no real person, surely, but a part of the picture, a figure painted into the grey landscape to give the final touch of tranquil life! But as the figure drew nearer and became more real, Foley began to wonder, who could it be who seemed so familiar to him?

"Why, Sutton!" he called out, as he joined him, surprised at finding the American still at Oxford, "You still here?"

Sutton started, and then greeting Foley in his old reserved way, they paced together slowly on the garden path. After Foley had talked a little about his travels and work, he turned to his companion and said in a friendly way, "But tell me about yourself, Eliaphet, it's three years since I have seen you; what have you been doing, and when are you really going back to America?"

Sutton replied with all his old vagueness and reticence that he had stayed; he had found it necessary; he had not decided yet about going back.

"Probably you will be sorry to leave Oxford when the time comes?" Foley suggested, but the American did not answer.

Eliaphet was a good deal changed, Foley

thought when they parted; he seemed so much thinner and more melancholy looking, and his voice was almost like that of another person. What a difference a few years made!

### X.

Several times in the following days Foley met his friend again—indeed, they two just then seemed almost alone together in Oxford —and more than once, in the long summer afternoons, they walked together in a desultory way among the vacant streets and empty Colleges. Sutton was even more reserved than of old, but there was a charm in his silent company and in his affectionate, scrupulous knowledge of the place. Each of the churches, dim College chapels, and libraries was dear and familiar to him now; he had found remnants of Norman architecture, and little early Gothic windows in obscure old places which Foley, who had thought he knew Oxford so well, was forced to admit he had never visited. And even for the despised classicism, Sutton seemed to have a certain fondness, for everything that bore the stately quaint mark of the Stuart times—Laud's quadrangle at St. John's, and its Italian-looking busts and arches; the chapel at Trinity; the little Ashmolean museum, and the prim old Botanic garden, with its battered statue of Charles I. over the gate, the half neglected formality of its urns and fountain, its walls and walks within.

Then the old names of places seemed all to have a meaning for him. He could trace the remains of the Religious Houses, the Friars Minor, the Friar Preachers, the Carmelites, after which some of the more ancient streets are called; showing Foley the gateways or ruined arches, bits of College buildings which now alone remain of their former stately precincts. And on their walks together Sutton often chose by preference the little back streets, or those ancient footpaths that wind through the old heart of the city, through the mediaeval town whose gables and walls and gardens still sleep in the sun, almost untouched, behind the modern fronts and the traffic of many of the busy streets.

To Foley in his sentimental mood just then, the quiet of Oxford was very pleasant, after the noise of the London season; and there seemed to be something almost poetic in the life of this solitary student. How wise he was after all, Foley thought, to stay there among the old colleges and churches, where the ambitions and obligations of the world could scarcely trouble him; nor the noise of its busy life break in on his tranquil

# The Youth of Parnassus

moods, or disturb the old memories he loved. And yet a vague suspicion crossing his mind, once or twice, made him ask himself, was Sutton really so happy after all?


## XI.

One morning this vacation quiet of the College was rather noisily broken by the arrival of a number of undergraduates, who had returned to prepare for an examination, bringing with them the noise and influences of the outside world. Now the American was no longer to be met with in the garden or quadrangle, whither he had been wont to come almost every day, as if fond of the place and not averse from Foley's company. Wondering that he did not see him any more, Foley one evening asked the undergraduates if they knew Sutton or had ever heard anything about him.

By sight and reputation they knew him very well,—a solitary person, who led in Oxford a most melancholy life, without friends or apparent occupation; staying there, it was reported, because of something in his past which kept him from going back to America.

Foley knew how distorted gossip of this kind would grow in coming through the minds of undergraduates; and yet there was enough in what they told, to make him uneasy about his friend. Sutton had given up studying theology, had tried history, making however a complete failure in the schools; he was said to have adopted strange religious ideas and had been heard, it was rumoured, groaning and scourging himself at night. There was a report too that some Americans had come to

Oxford, and, after visiting him, had gone to the Warden and accused Sutton of keeping some money which was not his own.

## XII.

As soon as he could, Foley went off to find his friend, getting the address from the College books. At last in a dark alley he discovered the house. Mr. Sutton had gone away from Oxford the day before, the landlady told him, and had not said when he would be back. Perhaps the gentleman would like to leave his card? The room was at the top; he must be mindful of the stairs. Climbing up with care, Foley opened the door and lighted a match in the darkness; the poverty and destitution of the little room growing vivid for a moment, and then fading again into blackness, affected him somewhat sadly. Just two chairs, a table, a bed, and a few signs of human habitation,—several books, a coat hanging on the wall, and three photographs over the fireplace, the familiar one of Dr. Turnpenny, the dreamy face of Philip Gerard, and a picture that Foley was touched to recognize as his own. All the pictures of Parnassus City, his class mates, the young lady, the street, and college, had disappeared, and a few old religious prints were in their place.

Feeling as if he had intruded where he had no right, Foley turned away; lingering on the stairs, however, for he was loth to leave the house till he had learned something more definite about his friend. Then in the hall below he met the landlady, and began to talk to her about the American. Mr. Sutton was such a kind gentleman, she said, and always very quiet; but lately he had been, she thought, very lonesome and melancholy, and he didn't seem to have any friends in Oxford now. And though he had paid her regular, she couldn't complain of that, yet she was afraid the poor gentleman had very little money. Indeed, he had seemed to be in some trouble, and now he had gone away mysterious-like. The voice of this woman, plainly so poor herself, her anxiety on Sutton's account, remained in Foley's mind in a haunting way. And yet, what could have happened, he asked himself, unable in common sense to imagine any definite trouble, and nevertheless disturbed by a sense of mystery, as if he had suddenly found himself face to face with something more real and sad than most of the sentiments and troubles of his own experience.

Certainly the American had greatly changed —the narrow, rustic young man who had come there first, and the pale scholar Foley had met years afterwards, in the twilight of the garden —there was difference enough between the two! he thought, putting them side by side in memory. But what this change was Sutton had not told; probably never would tell, for in his reserve and reticence he was just the same.

And yet in his letters he had written with much less reserve, Foley remembered. He began to wonder whether, if he should read the letters again, with more attention, he might not find in them some hint of Sutton's trouble. Friendless as the American seemed to be in Oxford, a little advice and sympathy from some one who understood his circumstances, might make perhaps all the difference to him.

When Foley got back to his own rooms, he began looking through the portfolio of papers that he had brought with him from

Germany. Yes, there they were, the envelopes addressed in Sutton's neat fine writing. Arranging them in order of their dates, he began to go through them. Letters written during two or three years of his friend's life, in half an hour he could read them all.


## XIII.

First came the letters Foley remembered: Sutton's first Long Vacation; his home-sickness in Oxford; his thoughts of Parnassus; the American tourists he would watch and speak with sometimes. Then in the autumn his impression of the chapel, his growing fondness for Oxford, followed by the sudden determination to go home, from which Dr. Joseph had dissuaded him, telling him that there was nothing he need be afraid of in Oxford, or in the Past.

Then came the letters which had come to Foley in the East, and been hardly regarded by him in the hurry of travel. Letters which read pleasantly for the most part, as he went through them now, with their echoes of charming Oxford life—charming for a time, though troubled afterwards. With Dr. Joseph's theology to rely on, and Dr. Joseph's approval of his life, Sutton's uneasy conscience had been at rest for a while, and he had let himself enjoy life without questioning—just the simple human joy of the world and youth, with the weather growing warmer, and the Spring blossoming in the gardens of that beautiful old city, where he was quite at home now.

"I have so enjoyed the Spring," he wrote "your tardy, veering English Spring, with its gusts of snow and black weather, and yet enough warm days to woo from the earth the

English flowers that till last year I only knew of in books. But I greet them as old friends now, the primroses, and cowslips, and daffodils. . . . May is here, the air is full of the greenness of leaves and the songs of birds, the lank rose trees are budding on the Gothic walls, and when I breathe the fragrant air and look about me I rub my eyes, and wonder whether May was ever so beautiful at home. Some beautiful days, of course, I can remember vividly; but I lived then for the most part, I think, among pale thoughts and theories, growing old before I was young, and looking so rarely out—indeed, thinking somehow that it was almost wrong to look out on the beauty and colour of the world. . . ."

He had written a good deal about Oxford; and really it wasn't true, what Foley had told him once, that he didn't deserve to live in so beautiful a place; he did care, and was learning more and more to look at things and enjoy them. On May morning he had gone to Magdalen to hear them salute the rising sun from the tower. "I wish I could describe it all," he wrote, "the streets, as I went out, cold and vacant in the early dawn, the pale flames in the street lamps, and the silence of those rows of sleeping houses, only broken, as I passed under garden walls, by the acute music of the birds awake already in the trees. Birds, millions of them! I never heard such a clamour. At the College gate there was a group of shivering people; and soon they let us in, to climb the steep tower stairs, with its narrow windows here and there in the darkness, with views like little old pictures of grey castles and green country. On the windy platform at the top we found almost all the College gathered, the President, and Fellows, and undergraduates, with the group of white choristers. Gradually, as we waited, the formless sky all round and above us grew white and blue; the sky-line reddened; and then, bringing a sudden hush in the crowded talk, a sudden baring of all our heads, the May sun began to blaze in the East; and as it rose into the sky the boys, facing the light, chanted loud, with their shrill young voices, the old Latin hymn. Well, you can hardly imagine what a solemn moment it was, with the slow hymn, the stately yellow sun rising over all that great view of green country. Turning toward Oxford we saw black figures like dots on the sun-flushed towers and roofs of the other Colleges. Our tower, and, indeed, the whole sky, seemed to rock with the pealing bells; and the undergraduates, engaging in a wild scuffle, tore off each other's caps and gowns, throwing them out into the air, to fall with giddy swirls on the roofs, or into the street below. It seemed almost an outburst of Pagan turbulence, after the Pagan sun-worship, up there on that windy tower-top over the sleeping town! I wrote describing it to Dr. Turnpenny; I only hope he won't be shocked!"

## XIV.

In Sir Philip Gerard, whom Foley had known slightly as a youth, of poor and ancient Catholic family, Sutton, it appeared, had found a congenial companion; and he described how they would often spend their afternoons together on the river; rowing up the windings of the Cherwell, past little woods and garden walks, or between the sliding horizons of meadow banks, where the tangled edge of grass and flowers fringed the near sky. "I lie on luxurious cushions in the bow, and Gerard pushes me along, through sleepy sunshine and shadow, and under the unwilling branches of trees ; and then, anchoring in some secluded place, we read together some poet or old book, while the endless afternoon glides by, and boats float down the shady river."

"This sounds dreadfully lazy, I'm afraid! But I am taking a rest ; I have been feeling rather tired, and Dr. Joseph says I had better do nothing but enjoy myself for a week or two now. . . ."

". . . I discovered the other day the old market. I wonder if you know it? It is a delightful place! People from the villages about Oxford have stalls there, and you see the ruddy, old-fashioned cottagers' wives, seated each one behind a fresh bank of vegetables and flowers she herself has grown at home in her quaint garden. Sweet, old-fashioned flowers, flags and peonies and roses, made up into tight bouquets and set out for sale in trim rows, not unlike, I fancy, the trim rows in which they grew in their formal cottage flower beds. . . ." Letters came to him from home, he said, telling of all that was going on in Parnassus City: the Bryant Literary Society they had started, the church bazaar for the missionary work, the Monday evening prayer meetings at the College; and he often felt that he ought to be back there, that he was dreaming away his time. Yes, it was like a dream in Oxford; but such an enchanted dream! . . .

He wrote, in another letter, of the Oxford bells. More and more he was conscious of them, sounding always in the near or distant sky; and if ever he woke up in the night, restless with his dreams, he had only to wait a little and they would ring out—first the silver voices of the Colleges, and then the slow booming tones of the great church, so near at hand. And he found a comfort, he said, in the nearness of the churches, and their wakefulness through the night.

Although of course he did not approve, he said, of a religion of external forms, yet he confessed that he had come to take a certain interest in noticing how, almost every time he went out, he discovered some new symbol of the old Catholic religion—old stone crosses, statues gazing out from the towers, images of the Virgin, hands raised in prayer, the adoration of kings and queens in the painted windows; and even in the gardens stone fragments, covered with ivy, of old saints—everywhere tokens of ancient faith, and intimations of another world, shining and immanent, about this world of sense. It was curious, but he had never noticed these

## 52 The Youth of Parnassus

things when he had first come to Oxford! Indeed, he grew to love all the antiquity of the place; was no longer oppressed or frightened by it; and for the old portraits in the hall and library, the tombstones in the cloisters, with their quaint epitaphs and names, he felt a certain fondness, he said, looking on the dead now, not as enemies, frowning on his creed and life, but as friends rather, and kindly predecessors.

### XV.

The lives of many of those old scholars and worthies had become familiar to him, since he had read Anthony à Wood's *Athenae Oxonienses*, and he had gone sometimes with his friend on antiquarian walks about Oxford, and the colleges Wood described. Or Gerard would lend him a horse, and they would ride out to visit the historic places and villages that lie in the old country about—Woodstock, Cumnor, Abingdon—the names were familiar to him of long date; had he not first read of some of them, and the scenes they were famous for, in Jones' *Excelsior Reader*, out in Indiana as a boy?

He spoke of the village churches, that seemed so beautiful on those June afternoons, as they stood among their old trees and flowers, with the white clouds in the sky above, a shiver of wind in the long grass over the graves. And then, through the scent of roses about the open door, the dim interior, with its white Norman arches, and light falling from painted windows on the crusaders' tombs —on all the many monuments of the dead. The dead! Sutton wrote that he had always known of the times gone by, and the faith of the Middle Ages, but only in an unreal way, through books. And it made such a difference—to him at least—if he saw the proof of a thing, actually existing with the daylight on it!

"Once, Gerard says, these churches were filled in the morning and evening light with labouring people kneeling in silent prayer. But that, of course, was in the Dark Ages. Gerard thinks that the world has done nothing but go back since the Middle Ages; certainly he does hate everything that is modern. How he will detest Parnassus City, if he comes to see me there, as he says he will. It has been bad for him, I am sure, living out of the world, as he has lived, among old memories and dreams of his own. He is a Catholic, you know, but he respects my religion; he knows, of course, what my views are, and we never talk about theology. There is a friend of his I meet sometimes a priest, and I suppose a Jesuit. But he seems really quite a cultivated person."

Foley took up another letter: They had ridden out, Sutton wrote, to an old country house and park, where Charles I. had stayed once, while Parliament was being held in Oxford. The house, all save one wing, now a farm-house, had been torn down; but on the hill overlooking the lake, in the midst of the green shade of beeches, the chapel was still standing, abandoned now, and almost untouched, save by decay and time, since the polite court of the Stuarts had said their worldly devotions there. What rich brocades, what hushed gallantries and frivolous prayers had once rustled and whispered under the graceful high arches of those pews! But birds had their nests there now, he said, while through the decaying roof the rain dripped down on the frail woodwork, the classic columns and fading colours of this deserted place of elegant worship and old fashion.

The American Puritan confessed to a certain tenderness for the generous lost cause, for the fine futile courage of the gay Cavaliers and lovely forgotten ladies. And as they rode homeward through the twilight, his companion sang snatches of some old Cavalier songs—tunes with a certain pathos and grace in their gallant wistful music.

## XVI.

Then there was a long letter, dating from the autumn after this delightful summer, in which he wrote again about Anthony à Wood, the old Oxford antiquary. He had been reading Wood's diaries, finding in them, he said, in spite of their old-fashioned pedantry and long genealogies, a vivid picture of the University

# The Youth of Parnassus

and Wood's life in it, two hundred years ago. A calm life, Sutton described it, in curious contrast to the times in which Wood lived, when the academic quiet was so often disturbed by armies, and royal visits, and great events; and the noise of tumults in the Oxford streets, and troops marching by, reaching the old antiquary's ears, would draw him from the chronicles of the past, to look with blinking eyes from his library window on the turmoil and disquiet of contemporary history. For his life was spent in his own study, or in "Bodlie's Library," or among the dusty archives of the Colleges, reading and transcribing the monastic registers, the old manuscripts and histories. Sutton quoted from his diary a sentence in which he speaks of the exceeding pleasure he took in "poring on such books."

"Heraldry, musick, and painting did so

much crowd upon him, that he could not avoid them, and could never give a reason why he should delight in those studies more than in others, so prevalent was nature." " My pen cannot enough describe," he writes in his enthusiasm, when he first read Dugdale's *Antiquities of Warwickshire*, " how A. Wood's tender affections and insatiable desire of knowledg were ravish'd and melted down by the reading of that book. What by music and rare books that he found in the public library, his life at this time and after was a perfect Elysium."

" Wood often went for long, solitary walks, collecting arms and monumental inscriptions from the churches, and visiting all the ruined religious Houses and old halls in the country about Oxford. He describes in his diary how, as he returned towards Oxford in the evening, 'after he had taken his rambles about the country to collect monuments,' he would hear the bells of Merton, his own College, ringing clearly in the distance."

"Wood had small love for the Puritans," Sutton wrote, "who in his lifetime were so long in power; and in his record of contemporary events, sudden deaths, and alleged appearances of the devil, he more than once mentions their destruction of antiquities, their contempt for the Fathers and Schoolmen, and hatred of all authority, and 'everything that smelt of an Academy, never rejoicing more than when he could trample on the gowne, and bring humane learning and arts into disgrace.'"

"Then came the Restoration, and almost the last event that Wood records is the revival of Catholicism under James II. Wood himself was suspected of being a Papist; his writings had made him enemies, and before he died he was expelled from the University, and his book burned by order of the Vice-Chancellor's Court."

"And yet, on the whole, his life was a happy one," Sutton said, writing, it was plain, with a certain envy for the tranquil occupations and lettered tastes of the old Oxford antiquary.

## XVII.

The next two letters that Foley found (and they were the last) were dated in the Long Vacation, nearly a year later. Either Sutton had not written again for some time, or Foley had lost the letters. It was the American's third summer in England; as before, he had stayed in Oxford. He described the quiet afternoons he spent in the College garden; how he seemed to be alone with Oxford and the past, and how even the city noises, which came in over the walls—the rattle of carts, the shrill, faint voices of newsboys, crying the world's events—only added a deeper hush to the stillness and solitude within, the sunlight on the grass, the shadows of the trees.

He remembered how homesick he had been the first summer he had spent in Oxford, and how he had longed to go back. But now that his work was almost finished, and he was soon to go to America, he could not help admitting that he shrank a little from it—felt a certain reluctance, after all. He would watch, as he had watched before, the tourists who now and then came into the quiet garden. Then he had enjoyed seeing them, and wished he could talk to them; but now . . . !

And one day some people whom he had known in Indiana came in. He spoke to them, showed them about, and tried to be friendly, and yet they seemed so far away somehow! He hated himself for it, and tried to believe that it was all the fault of Oxford and its fastidious standards; he had let himself be too much influenced, but when he got back to Parnassus again, he hoped he should see things as he used to see them, and feel the same towards the Slocums and all his old friends.

But in the last letter, "It will never be the same now," Sutton had written; "I have come too far and stayed too long. At first I was always thinking of Parnassus City; I would dream of it at night, and wake in the morning to wonder at the strangeness of my dim little windows and the voices of the rooks outside. But then it began to fade, and gradually everything changed. And yet, poor fool that I was, all the time I tried to think that I was preparing myself to go back. Of course I *shall* go back; if I can't be a Minister, I can still teach in their university, perhaps—I *must* do something to help them, it would be treachery if I did not. But my heart will be far away from it all, I know. I try to think of the excellent people there, and how fatally kind they have been to me; but when I shut my eyes, I can see nothing but the ugly church, the wooden 'university,' and a great sun-baked street, with sparse houses and dusty trees straggling off on the prairie. How can I ever live there now? And yet, if I had never come away, I might have been happy. Why did they send me to Oxford, I wonder. Yet was it not my fate? It seems to me that I *must* have come here sometime!"


## XVIII.

With this the letters ended. From the undergraduates Foley had heard how Sutton tried to study history, but failed rather badly in it. What had happened afterwards he had not heard, save by vague report. He only knew that Sutton was still in Oxford.

But no wonder he had stayed there, Foley thought, remembering the passion for the place that breathed in Sutton's letters, his growing preoccupation with, and interest in, everything that was ecclesiastical and ancient. Indeed, the beauty and antiquity of Oxford, the libraries and cloisters and old places he haunted, now seemed to have grown into an almost necessary part of the American's environment, the needful background of his life. As if, like old Anthony à Wood, one could not imagine him living anywhere except in Oxford, walking through its almost doorless streets, or on the lawns of its College gardens, and ordering his studies and ways by the sound of its bells. Why then should he not stay there;

was it anything more than a false conscience that had made him feel he ought to go back to America?

The next morning, as if in answer to this question, Foley received an unexpected visit from Abel, Dr. Joseph's assistant. He had come, he said, to find out where Sutton was; they were a good deal worried about him; they must be allowed to see him again before he took any step. Foley was greatly surprised at the way Abel spoke; he knew nothing of the American's whereabouts, he said; they had told him at his lodgings the night before that he was away from Oxford.

"Yes, I know, I saw your card there. But I supposed you would know where he has gone, or would be willing to tell me how I could find out. We have heard again from America, and really, for your own sakes you must allow us to see him once."

With still greater astonishment Foley protested that he knew nothing; he had feared Sutton might be in trouble, but having just returned, after two years abroad, he had no idea of what the trouble was. His assurances were so evidently sincere, that Abel, who had looked at him suspiciously at first, now shut the door and came forward into the room. The trouble was that Sutton had absolutely refused to go back to America. They might have known it would happen, he added; and, in answer to a question of Foley's, he gave his version of all that had occurred.

Sutton had come to Oxford with a letter from Dr. Turnpenny, his pastor and guardian, requesting Dr. Joseph to see that he should live under some kind of care and protection. Dr. Joseph, as their own buildings were not yet finished, had arranged with the Warden of St. Mary's that the young man should enter that College and live there, while he carried on his theological work with his own tutors.

It was a mistake; Abel had thought it a mistake all along. With another man it might not have mattered; but Sutton, thrown into the society of rich young men, who had no sympathy with his ideas, and who ridiculed his ways, had not been able to withstand their influence. And just when he was on the point of ordination, he had thrown it all over; said he no longer believed in Methodism, or wished to be a minister. He had stayed for another year in Oxford, studying, or pretending to study, history; but he could not have worked very seriously; the examiners said, indeed, that his papers were full of the most absurd ideas. And now he refused to go back to America at all. Abel didn't know who it was who had tried to pervert him; it was reported to be the Jesuits—and there was a man called Gerard, Sir Philip Gerard—; but at any rate they ought to know what trouble they had made.

Foley said he was certain there had been no deliberate attempt to pervert Sutton. If any of his friends had tried to influence him, it was probably because they believed in culture, and thought it would help him in his work.

"Help him to be a minister out in Indiana! How could the ideas of a narrow university set and its expensive tastes help a man for that?"

"But everyone surely was the better for being cultivated!" Foley exclaimed.

Even to this Abel could not agree entirely; he admitted that of course culture had its charm and value; only in cases it might be dangerous, he thought. But how could that be? Foley asked, and for a moment, in their discussion of the larger question, they almost forgot Sutton. Abel thought that an undue cultivation of taste, of the sense of beauty, without an equal training of the reason, would make you into a narrow and fastidious person, judging things by the eyes and ears, and caring only for what was well-expressed and beautiful. And surely for the most part, he said, (and he seemed anxious to be fair and moderate,) for the most part it was the ideals of the past, the out-worn, romantic, and old-fashioned things, that had had time to be well-expressed, while the modern— "But all this has very little to do with Sutton!" he said, stopping suddenly.

"Oh, I don't know, isn't he the kind of person you mean—a sensitive poetic person—"

"Eliaphet Sutton! he never wrote poetry, did he?"

"No, I don't mean exactly that. Only it seems to me natural enough that a man of his temperament, coming to Oxford from an ugly new town, should not want to go back."

"Temperament!" Abel exclaimed, as if the word annoyed him. Then more quietly he added that he did not think anything could excuse Sutton for behaving in the way he had behaved. Why he himself had come to Oxford from a new town that was probably as ugly as Parnassus City. They were angry enough in Parnassus, you couldn't talk of temperaments out there! It had really broken Dr. Turnpenny's heart. "If you could only see his letters! No, after spending all the old man's money—"

"His money?" Foley asked.

"Yes, didn't you know? He was sent over on a subscription got up by the Methodist church there, and Dr. Turnpenny, who had adopted him and brought him up, gave all his savings. He was to go back of course, and help support Dr. Turnpenny. He was engaged to a girl out there too. And now he says he won't go back. But really he must, it doesn't matter what he says. It's the only honest and decent thing for him to do."

"Indeed he must go back," exclaimed Foley. "I hadn't the least idea!—"

### XIX.

Foley went to Sutton's rooms again, but for several days he could hear nothing of him. One evening, however, when he was sitting in the garden, happening to look up, he saw the melancholy figure of the American coming down the garden path. Now that he actually saw Sutton, and was vividly aware of the atmosphere of reserve and solitude that enveloped him, Foley shrank from saying the things that he felt he ought to say. And yet someone must speak to him; someone must tell him his duty, and make him go back to the good simple people who had cared for him, supported him, and who relied on him so much!

He had been away, Sutton said, as the two young men walked slowly down the garden path. It was very still there in the twilight; and they were alone, shut in as it seemed, and very remote from the world outside.

"Have you decided yet when you are going home?" Foley asked.

"Home?"

"Yes; home to America."

"I don't know," Sutton replied. After a moment he added, in the same quiet voice, "perhaps I shall never go back."

"Then you have found some occupation in England?"

Sutton shook his head.

But didn't he think he ought to go back then, Foley asked. One had duties—and, trying to speak more lightly, he added, "You must have learned a great deal, Eliaphet, after studying all these years. Oughtn't you to go back and teach them out there?"

"I have nothing to teach them—nothing they would be willing to learn."

"Oh, but surely, if you tried you could find something! It seems to me you *ought* to try."

"Oh, I *have* tried!" he said, his cheeks flushing with painful emotion; "but now they don't want me to come back any more— they never want to see me again! I used to pray I might never change;—and when you would argue with me,—but now I see it was all wrong, and all my liberal ideas—"

"I hope," Foley interrupted, for this had

been on his conscience ever since his talk with Abel, "I hope your change, whatever it is, has nothing to do with anything I ever said; you must have misunderstood me," and he went on to explain that he had never been really reactionary. He had always believed in compromise, and a conservative, reasonable progress.

"Do you know, Eliaphet," he went on, "I think you have made a mistake in staying here so long in this old place. It isn't wholesome to live so far from real life; you ought to get away, you ought to go home."

But Sutton had only listened to two or three of his friend's words. "No," he cried eagerly, "no, we can make no compromise. We must give up the human reason, we must go back to the Past, we must submit. Oh, Foley," he cried, and there was a strange appeal in his voice, "we have been friends, but now we may never see each other again, —let me warn you, you must decide whether you will be on the right or the wrong side— oh, if you only knew at what peril you refuse to listen!"

For a moment Foley was almost frightened. Then, reminding himself of reason and reality, he said, "But, Eliaphet, are you quite sure that you yourself are doing what is right in staying here? When so much depends on you out there—Dr. Turnpenny and all. And they have sacrificed so much too. Have you thought—"

"As if I was not always thinking of it!" Sutton cried; "but I could not go back to them a Roman Catholic; they would rather I was dead. And Foley, when you judge me, remember that I have had to make sacrifices too—I have given up everything, everything! What can I do?"

# The Youth of Parnassus

A Roman Catholic! Of course he could not go back. Foley was dismayed. Why had he not foreseen it?

For a moment they stood in silence. Then Sutton turned away.

"You don't understand," he said, in a voice that his friend always remembered afterwards; "No one understands," and he went down the path alone and out of Foley's sight.

## XX.

When Foley went the next day to Sutton's lodgings, he was told that Sutton had already left Oxford; had gone away early that morning. Where he had gone, however, no one seemed to know. Certainly Foley never found out; he never saw Sutton again, nor, in spite of all his inquiries, did he ever hear anything but the most vague and uncertain news about him. Abel said he had never gone back to Parnassus City. And then, years after, it was reported that an Oxford man, when visiting some old shrine in Italy, had recognized, or thought he recognized, Sutton in the monk who showed him about the church.

Foley never got rid of a certain feeling of remorse, a sense that at the beginning he had too lightly interfered in the life of the young Dissenter.

But then he would tell himself, that it was probably after all nothing less than Oxford itself, with its old ways and memories, that had gradually changed and influenced the American. Influenced him not for good, surely! he thought. And indeed, remembering Sutton's slow estrangement from his early ideas and friends, his poor attempts to remain faithful, the trouble and mystery in which he had disappeared at last, Foley would ask himself, (and he took a strange sort of pleasure in the question,) whether there were not something really dangerous in the venerable and Gothic beauty of Oxford, a chill in the old shadows, an iron sound in the bells.

# *The Will to Live*
## Part One

# The Will to Live

## I.

"MORAL Philosophy," notwithstanding all its modern ideas and developments, is still taught at Oxford from the Greek texts of Plato and Aristotle. Something indeed of the old Academic discipline might be said still to exist there, the tradition of it coming down through the Schools of the Middle Ages. Certainly the discussions between tutor and pupils, by means of which so much of the philosophic training is carried on, are not without a certain resemblance to the Socratic dialogues. And the young men who are so eager and amusing in Plato's writings—one might find the like of these, perhaps, among the English undergraduates, as well as the types with which modern novels have made us more familiar. The questions they talk and think about would at least be much the same as those so eagerly debated in the Athenian garden—the old questions about Truth and Justice and Beauty; and then the meaning or purpose of Life—that question which is the oldest of all, and which each generation of youth tries to solve in some new way.

. . . . . . . .

"Good night, sir"—"Good night"—"Good night"—and their discussion ended, the young men took their caps and books, and clattered noisily down the stone staircase from the tutor's room. They still lingered a moment, outside in the quadrangle, four or five together, vaguely talking in the darkness.

"Ames was right, you know—what he said about Pleasure."

"Old Ames! what does he know about it?" Waters interrupted. More than once, during the argument that evening, Waters had dropped a book or shuffled his feet impatiently; and now, declaring that all such talk was great waste of time and "rot" anyhow, he went off, after vainly inviting the others to join him, to an interrupted game of cards. In a minute the others separated, some to work, one or two to the concert in the college hall. Walter Cornish walked away alone across the quadrangle. Finding a bench, he sat listlessly down, his hands in his pockets, his feet stretched out in front of him. He would do no more work that night; it would be better to rest there for a while, listening to the music of the concert.

Cornish, with the others, would be in for his last examinations in a few weeks; then he would be leaving Oxford. But as he had money enough of his own, and belonged moreover to that fortunate class of young Oxford men to whom success at everything seems easy, he could look into the future, untroubled by most of those commonplace difficulties and despairs that beset the ordinary unknown, untried, young man, when he is leaving the university to go out into the world.

It seemed very hot that evening; no breath of air was stirring within the enclosure of those trees and walls. From the open windows of the college hall tinkling piano notes came faintly now and then across the darkness; while, drifting in over the roofs of the college, and deadening at times the music, there came, like a dim smoke of sound, the rumour of city noises, of carts, footsteps, and high faint voices in the street outside. But as Cornish sat there lazily, his hands deep in his pockets, his eyes fixed on the ground, he soon ceased to hear either the music or the sounds of the streets. Vagrant thoughts about himself, his own affairs and prospects, were going through his head. Then phrases from their argument—Pleasure wasn't the End, and the End wasn't Pleasure; but whose pleasure, and the end of what? To his tired mind, however, the words were little more than empty sounds. Other things he had been studying floated past in large dim masses; he remembered the armies, invasions, and old battles of history; the Roman Empire seemed to be near him, like something immense and heavy in the night. And behind it in the past were the Persian, Assyrian, Egyptian Dominations, with the weight of all their millions and millions of lives!

He was going to do well in the examinations, he knew; more or less mechanically he repeated over what his tutor had said, and some flattering words the Warden had written to his father—"We consider him one of our best men; he is certain to distinguish himself."

"But what's the good of it all?" he found himself asking. He looked up at the college buildings, dark about him, save for their squares of yellow windows. Gradually he began to wake out of his vacant reverie. What was the good of doing well?—why, it was an absurd question; of course, he wanted to do well, to win honour for himself and his College. He assured himself of this, in conventional phrases, but somehow, just then, he did not seem to care in the least for success like that, and honour. Yet here he had been, all this time, working for nothing else!

He was ashamed of this want of ambition,

## The Will to Live

this deadness of desire. Of course, there were other things he cared for, he told himself, and to prove this he brought to mind the interests and pleasures of his ordinary life—his friendships, the ideas and books he believed in, his public speaking, the positions he held in various societies. But somehow all these seemed utterly foolish, futile, and unimportant. In desperation he began to think of simpler things—of boating, good clothes, and horses, and some riding boots he was having made. But everything, even the most universal pleasures of life, struck him now as tasteless and absurd. Why did people do such things, and what could they find in them to enjoy?

"But it's against common sense to feel this way!" he said to himself. He had always thought the disillusions of youth somewhat ridiculous, and often had made fun of the modern philosophy, or pseudo-philosophy, of disenchantment, with its literature of passion and despair. And now, as he sat there in the familiar quadrangle, with the rooms of his friends about him, all the people he knew so well, in there at the concert, he was uncomfortably aware of how absurd they would think it, should they know that he too had secretly begun, in the old, foolish, hackneyed way, to meditate on the nothingness of life. He of all people, who had always taken such sensible, commonplace views of things!

"Well, it will be different soon; I shall have things to work for that really are worth while," he told himself. Hitherto, when he had felt any futility in his life, he had put it down to the youthfulness of his occupations, feeling sure that the world beyond his school or college, with its great interests and ambitions, would give endless objects of desire. But now, in spite of himself, he could not help asking—what were those great interests and ambitions after all?

Almost comically there rose before his mind pictures of all the middle-aged people he knew —his relatives, his father's friends—large, solemn, successful people, who were thought, and thought themselves, very important. And the dull speeches they made, and the way they often grew red and angry, as they argued about the Government, or the Eastern question! And their houses, their wives and dinner parties, their social differences and ambitions, and the way they pushed and struggled for money and titles! What was the value of it all; to succeed or fail, what difference did it make? He tried to imagine himself at the head of what would be his profession, as Lord Chancellor—a fat and bald Lord Chancellor in stuffy robes—wasn't that the position that young men were supposed to be ambitious of attaining? Or if he should make a fortune, or write a famous book, or carry some great reform through Parliament? But, somehow, he did not seem to care; and gradually, as he listened to the far-off rumour of the city, it came to sound faintly in his ears like a voice of blind craving —as if the agitation of the world and life were meaningless and vain. And he would go out into it, he knew, would struggle and push with the others. . . .

Now from the open windows, sounds of music floated again across the quadrangle. He could picture to himself the audience, all those rows of young men, sitting there in the hot air and gaslight. Indeed, he could almost see, he felt, into the rows of minds— if you could call them minds—behind all those heads: the ridiculous images of hope and cheap romance wakened by the music, the

## The Will to Live

foolish dreams of the future, and false, poetic ideas of life.

Pity the poets and novelists could not invent something a little more true to life! Cornish thought. For after all they had but two receipts: either they enlarged the world into a glorious and unreal place, full of love, success, and eternal sunshine, or else they magnified poor human nature, and invented towering, Byronic heroes, who could find nothing in a shrunken universe worthy of their passionate souls.

The music finished in a noise of long and loud applause. How all of them enjoyed it; how all of them believed in it, he thought; finding something foolish and inane in these sounds of clapping hands and pounding feet. A little while afterwards the concert ended, and the audience, a vague press of people, began to murmur and move down the steps of the hall, and pass him in the darkness. But now the sound of their footsteps and cheerful retreating voices came back to him almost sadly. A whole generation of youth, they seemed to him, as he sat there almost like some remote spectator—a whole generation of youth, those young men, pouring out of that ancient hall and passing away into the silence.

They were all gone at last; one by one the bright windows in the hall grew dark. Cornish still sat there alone. These voices and footsteps and dim figures, moving past him thus in the darkness, had left his mind curiously vibrating. So life went by, he thought, a few careless steps together on the brief-trodden path, a few words, a few greetings, and then the darkness and silence of death. What a curious mystery it was, this life, so vivid and brief in each of those passers by; the life he was conscious of in himself, as he sat there alone—the sound of his breath, the blood beating at his temples, the "soul" within—what was the meaning of it all, and for what reason was it given?

Surely this was the question of philosophy—the very question they had discussed that evening! And now, for the first time, he realized that the theories and systems he had been studying so long were not mere exercises of thought, and abstract speculations, but almost passionate attempts to explain the meaning of existence—of his own existence!

But the great solutions of the philosophers—Aristotle's "Contemplation," Kant's "Moral Law," the "Calculated Pleasure" of the Hedonists, and all the rest—there seemed to be a mortal coldness in them all. Surely they could never give a motive, or make life desirable to anyone! Vaguely dismayed at this conclusion, he repeated over to himself all the words again. Still he could find in them no motive for existence; and in a dim way he began to feel half proud of this discernment. Yes, Waters had been right after all, (and somehow he pitied both Waters and himself), philosophy was but a barren waste. And the picture of a great desert filled his mind—a desert of endless sand.

. . . . . . . .

When he was again conscious of himself, for a moment he wondered where he was, confused by the discomfort of his position, and the coolness of the air. Then through the darkness he saw, outlined against the starry sky, the trees and buildings of the College quadrangle, and remembered how he had sat down there to rest after their discussion. He must have fallen asleep, and now it was late—the night had grown completely silent, and only one or two windows shone yellow in the blackness of the walls. What had their argument been about? he began to ask himself; but, chancing to look up again, he forgot everything in his wonder at the brilliance of the stars. The whole patch of sky, shut in by the dark College roofs, quivered and glowed with shining stars; he thought he had never seen the vault of heaven so wonderful and luminous.

The long, faint sigh of a passing train on the distant railway brought back his thoughts at last, out of their vague wonder, to the earth and himself again. His imagination wandered after the train as it went through the night towards London. Soon he would be in London himself, he thought, smiling. It was not three weeks now. There were some dances he was going to, and a cricket match, and the theatre, of course. . . .

But then a vague sense of misfortune weighed him down, and in a moment he remembered how, a little while before, he had decided that life was altogether inane and meaningless. How was it that he had grown so foolishly eager again? No secret had been revealed to him; he had found no meaning behind desire, no purpose in existence. Yet here he was, looking forward to dances, actually counting the days to a cricket match! It was absurd for a self-conscious spirit to desire such things as these, especially after surveying life and philosophy, and finding there was no reason why you should desire anything at all!

But somehow Cornish did not seem to need a reason now; success, love, friendship, and even dances and cricket matches, he desired these things for themselves, they shone with their own brightness; no theory, no sanction of Greek or German philosophy could possibly make him want them more. How was it that there were desires that reason did not give? He puzzled over this, till at last he saw the question was rather a meaningless one, a question of words only. For desire of life came long before reasoning about it; reason did not sit aloft in a purer air, creating out of itself the meanings of experience. It could create no desires, could give us indeed none of the ultimate facts of life, for the ideas it used were all abstracted from things our direct perceptions gave us. And the existence of these things themselves—the blue sky, the solid earth, the sweetness of youth and sunshine—it could never prove, it did not need to prove! When, a little while before, he had felt no desire, reason had not helped him. And now he did not want its help.

The striking clocks told Cornish the lateness of the hour, and he got up to go in. As he walked across the quadrangle he heard voices and laughter in the darkness, and dimly saw a group of young men come out of a doorway in front of him.

"Well, have you had a good game, Waters?" he asked, as he joined them.

"Oh, a ripping game. What have you been doing?"

"Nothing much—thinking."

"Thinking! Lord, I'd turn looney if I thought so much. What's the good of it? You'd much better have taken a hand."

Cornish laughed. "Well, I believe you're right," he said.

# The Will to Live
## Part Two

# The Will to Live

## II.

WILLIAM WATERS had dreamed that the Persians, in a fleet of Canadian canoes, had come up the Thames to attack the College barge, and that he himself had been sent on foot to demand reinforcements from the Oxford examiners at Sparta. And after the weary, breathless running, the hopeless search, in his dream, for the right Greek words, it was most delightful to open his eyes and find himself comfortably lying in his familiar bedroom, with the sunlight glowing on the blinds.

## The Will to Live

"Why am I so happy?" he asked himself, and then he remembered that it was all over now; for the future he would never have to trouble about Greek or examinations, or getting up in the morning, or any of their stupid rules and worries. For the future! As he lay there, lazily opening and shutting his eyes, vague, bright pictures of the life before him floated through his mind, and set his heart beating a little quicker.

William Waters was the son of a business man in a northern town, who, with some sacrifice, had sent him, the eldest son, to the University, in order that his education, and the connections he would form, might help him on in the world. Now that the young man, after a lucky scramble through the examinations, had just finished four pleasant years of Oxford life, it was his vague purpose to find some occupation in London, something pleasant and gentlemanly, which would enable him to live as he liked.

"Of course, sir, I know one can't expect anything very much at first," he said, half aloud, as he imagined himself talking modestly and sensibly to his tutor. For he was going to talk about it to Ames; old Ames wasn't such a fool about things of that kind. "There is no nonsense about that young Waters," Ames would say afterwards; "a modest, sensible chap, the kind of man who'll always do well." Waters was determined to do well of course; he would get on, he told himself, when people came to realize how hard he worked. And as the young man lay there in bed, he decided that in the future no one should ever accuse him of laziness and neglecting work. By simply making up his mind to it, he thought he would entirely change his character, and begin life anew, winning position and wealth by his own unremitting industry.

Buller and Antrobus would be in London, he told himself, and Philpotts, most likely, and they would belong to the same club, where they would go on Sunday mornings to smoke and read the sporting papers. He would work tremendously hard, of course, spending laborious nights over his books, but he would also go out a great deal into society. He would not be dissipated—he didn't care much for that—but still he would not be Puritanical either. He meant to be moral and steady, and at the same time he would enjoy the pleasures of a man of the world. But he would be always kind and popular; people in fashionable society would say that William Waters was such a good fellow, and in the Park ladies would smile at him from their carriages, and smart young men would walk with him arm in arm. And he would live well; but still he would save money, and would soon pay off his Oxford bills, and send money to his father. For he would always be very kind to his people, having his sisters to visit him, helping them to marry well (he himself meant to marry someone for love who was very rich), and sometimes he would give up parties at country houses in order to pay them visits at home. How his fur coat and knowledge of the great world would impress all the neighbours!

"But I must get up," Waters said to himself, remembering how he was to go and see his tutor and talk over plans. And after luncheon Buller was going to drive them out, three of them, with his tandem to Woodstock. And thinking vaguely of this drive, and of some new clothes that he meant to wear, Waters was just falling off to sleep again, when his bull-dog came rushing up the stairs, and began to whine and scratch at the door. Rousing himself, Waters jumped up, and went with a call of affection to the door to let Lo-Ben in.

After he had bathed and dressed himself in his new fresh-smelling clothes, the young man sauntered into the sitting-room of his lodgings, and rang the bell for breakfast. The day was bright; Waters felt wonderfully fresh and well; there were pleasant aches in his arms and legs as he moved, for the whole of the day before he had been rowing on the river.

After breakfast he was just sitting down to smoke his pipe comfortably, when, looking at his watch, he snatched up his cap and rusty gown, and started out towards College. By Jove! what a day it was! He walked along through the sunshine, smiling to himself, while Lo-Ben barked and bounced from side to side. It was a good world, Waters thought a good world, and now he was really going to enjoy it.

As Waters was tying up Lo-Ben in the College porch, he was seized on suddenly from behind.

"Come along, fat William," they cried, pulling and pushing him along, "we're going to have a little game—you must take a hand."

Twisting himself around, as he struggled, Waters recognized two of his friends, and appealed to reason breathlessly; he had to go and see old Ames, on his honour he had; he would look in afterwards, in about half-an-hour, and stay to luncheon if they liked. So he started across the quadrangle, looking back and smiling and shaking his head, as he dodged the bits of gravel with which they pelted him. It was a good place after all, the old College, Waters thought, when he was out of danger and could look about. He remembered the two years he had lived in rooms looking out on this quadrangle; the pleasant hours he had spent, sitting in the window with his pipe, or lying on the grass whole Sunday afternoons, lazily reading, or talking with his friends; he thought of the beautiful chapel, and the old hall that was so much admired, and how he had sat up a tree one evening and poured water on the Dean, and how at night the stealthy bonfires had blazed up red and sudden in the dark.

He was really sorry to leave the old place, he thought sentimentally, remembering the emotions he had read of as felt by young men in books when about to leave their school or college. But then, with healthy common-sense, he told himself that all they wrote in books about your college days, and life never being so happy afterwards, was damned nonsense. Waters knew how men lived in London!

"Sorry I'm late, sir," he said as he entered his tutor's room, addressing the spare shining head that was bent over a heap of papers.

Mr. Ames raised his worn, cynical, kind face, and looked at Waters with short-sighted eyes. "Oh, no matter, sit down won't you, Waters," and he gave a last hurried shuffle to his papers. Waters thought that Ames must spend his life looking for lost papers; and although occasionally surprised by flashes of almost supernatural knowledge in his tutor, for the most part he entertained—as a heathen might towards his helpless, yet vaguely awful, idol—a certain good-natured pity for the absent-minded, easily outwitted man.

"I thought I'd like to talk things over with you a little," Waters said, sitting down in a chair that groaned with his athletic weight. "I must decide what I shall choose, what to go in for."

"To go in for?" Ames repeated, looking at him vaguely.

"I mean, I must choose"; Waters found a pleasure in talking, not as an undergraduate, but as a serious young man. "One must do something of course."

"Of course it *is* better," Ames assented, though he still looked rather puzzled.

"I thought I'd talk to you about the Bar, or something of the kind."

Ames looked at him blankly. "Talk to me about the Bar?"

"Yes, I thought I'd better ask your advice."

"Do you mean for yourself?" Ames asked after a moment, "but I supposed—I always supposed you were going into your father's business; he has some business, hasn't he, or am I wrong?"

"Into my father's business!" Waters laughed comfortably. "No, I shouldn't ever think of that. No, I want to live in London."

"Oh, I see!"

"Yes, of course if anything very good was offered me somewhere else,—but no, I think I prefer London. What would you advise?"

"What I should advise!" Ames said, looking at him hopelessly. "I suppose you've thought of something for yourself; you have some preference?"

"Preference? Oh no, nothing special. I thought I'd ask you."

Again Ames looked at him with an odd expression. Then in his polite, weary, equable voice, he said, "Well, I must try and think. I suppose your father—what does he want you to do?"

"My father—!" Waters' voice showed what he thought of fathers. "Oh, he said that if

I had a university education, there would be something."

"Ah, did he! Well, I suppose he ought to know," Ames said doubtfully.

"Oh, he doesn't know of anything definite," Waters explained; and then, speaking loudly, as if to a deaf man, he added, "It was only what he thought."

"Ah, that's quite different, isn't it?" Ames exclaimed, his face brightening.

"But surely there is a great deal to do in London," Waters continued.

Yes, there must be a good deal, Ames admitted doubtfully; at least everyone seemed very much occupied there.

"All I want is some work, that isn't too much grind, and decent pay."

"Ah, that is all that most people want," Ames observed, with half a sigh.

"Of course at first I shouldn't expect anything very much," Waters went on, hardly heeding his tutor's vague remarks; and he explained again that he only wanted some decent occupation, with pay enough to live on. Then he waited, gazing at his tutor's blank face as one might gaze at a revolving lighthouse, waiting for its flash of light. As nothing came, however, he said, "Surely there are lots of places where they want Oxford men?"

"Possibly there were"; Ames looked as if he, however, had never heard of them.

"But Grant and Vaughan had got good places, and Sturdy, they said, was doing well at the Bar."

"Ah, I see you mean those clever men, who do so well in the Schools and all. You're quite right; a man like Cornish for instance; I thought you meant more the average man."

No, it wasn't Cornish, Waters meant; it wasn't the average man either. "I mean more the man—what you call an all-round-man."

"What I call an all-round-man?" Ames looked bewildered.

"I mean," Waters continued, with desperate efforts to explain himself, "I mean the man who is rather good all round, rows, and that sort of thing. Perhaps he didn't get a First; didn't care much what he got, didn't approve of the system."

Ames seemed busy looking for his glasses.

"There are people who don't approve of the system," Waters went on. "I read an article once by someone, Professor something, not approving of examinations. I forget just who it was."

"Professor Freeman, perhaps?"

"Yes, that's it! Well now, a man like

that, what is he going to do?" Waters asked, with renewed confidence.

"But Professor Freeman is dead, you know."

"But,—but,—I'm not speaking of Professor Freeman."

"How would you like to be a solicitor?" Ames asked, putting on his glasses.

"A solicitor! oh, I shouldn't care for that," Waters promptly replied. "You see it isn't the kind of work I like, and then the vacations are too short."

Ames said nothing. He was sitting unusually still, and his large glasses reflecting the light, resembled two enormous shining oval eyes in the smoothness of his face. What he was really looking at Waters could not tell, and he grew more and more uncomfortable. At last, with diminished confidence, "There *are* men who get on well at the Bar?" he said.

"There are."

"And if I were living in London I might do some writing? They do that, don't they?"

"They do." Then Ames sighed and shook his head. "I think you had better go home, Waters," he added; "I'm afraid there's nothing else. If you had spoken to me before, I should have told you this."

"Oh, good Lord, Mr. Ames, you don't mean there's nothing!" Waters sat up in his chair, with open mouth, staring at his tutor.

"Well, you know, I'm afraid there isn't."

"Oh but, Mr. Ames, there must be something!"

"Well you can try; but honestly, I think you had—if your father can have you—I think you had better go home."

Waters looked at him. "He knows I helped to paint his door red last week," the young man muttered to himself, "and now he's furious about it."

But the comfort of this ebbed away gradually, as Ames went on to describe the different professions, the struggle for success, the cruel competition. Ames indeed seemed to have focussed himself, and instead of the vague astonished way in which he was wont to speak of practical affairs, he now showed a precision, and clearness, and knowledge of life that was really appalling. "I am sorry it is so, Waters," he ended. "We live pleasantly here, and we almost forget what the world outside is like."

"I do think some one might have told me, Mr. Ames; I do indeed." Waters could have cried with disappointment.

"You would never have believed it, Waters; we none of us can believe that the world doesn't need us. It's hard, but whether we live or die, the world doesn't care, can get on perfectly well without us. We each have to find it out for ourselves." He sighed as if he too had once known youth and hope, and the indifference of the world.

"But, Mr. Ames, I can't go home, indeed I can't. My other brother was going into the business, and I always told people,—and everybody supposed,—and to think that all my time here is wasted."

"Oh, not exactly wasted," Ames answered kindly. "It will always help you, to be an Oxford man, and you will be sure to find it pleasanter at home than you expected." Then beginning again to look at his papers, he added, more in his old distant way, "I'll see you again, I hope, before you go down. They'll miss you in College," he added politely, as Waters moved towards the door. "I'm sure the 'Torpid'—"

"I might be a solicitor, Mr. Ames," Waters said in a meek voice, as he stood disconsolately, his hand on the door-knob.

"Well, talk it over with your father," Ames replied, without looking up. "It takes time and money you know. You think he wouldn't mind?"

"Oh no, he won't mind," Waters said, although he knew his father would mind very much indeed.

He walked away slowly through the familiar quadrangle. His father!—how would he ever dare tell his father? But no, it couldn't be true that there was nothing for him, that nobody wanted him. He was well known in College, had played in the football team, and rowed in the "Torpid," and people liked him. Besides it was such a thing, they always said, to be an English gentleman; and then Oxford culture—and you read of the successful careers of rowing men, how they became Cabinet Ministers, and Bishops, and things. No, it couldn't be true. . . .

"Poor Lo-ben," he said, patting his dog tenderly, as he unchained him in the porch. "Poor old Lo-ben, you'll stick to your master, won't you?" The dog whined and licked the young man's hand, and they went out into the street together.

Well, they would live alone, he and Lo-ben, and they would go out for lonely walks, after the long dreary days of work in his father's office. And the people there would see him, and wonder about him; but he would always be distant, only coldly polite when they met. Sometimes his old College friends would come to stay in the neighbourhood; but they would not look him up: all his friends would forget him, though he would always remember them. And that afternoon they would all drive off without him, probably they would be really glad not to have him. And they would be perfectly happy; but he would never be happy again.

For no, it was not true, what Ames had said, about his getting to like it at home. He would always hate it, he told himself desperately; and life and everything was hateful; there was a chill in the sunshine, the streets seemed full of noise and work and ugly working people. What was the good of it? he wondered. And Ames said it was all like that. What was the good of it, he asked again, when he flung himself down into one of the great easy chairs in his lodgings. If you had to live in a dirty provincial town, and sit on a stool all day, what was the good? Of course some of the men at home seemed happy enough; they had their cricket on Saturdays and things; but then they weren't university men. For himself, Waters decided, for the first time in his life considering in his concrete way the problem of existence, for himself it was all finished; there was nothing more in life which could give him pleasure.

The servant brought up luncheon. At first Waters thought he could eat nothing, and when he did begin in a melancholy way, he bitterly contrasted his lonely meal with the happy party in College. He felt an immense pity for himself; he would die young, he was sure; the life might even drive him to suicide —such things had happened.

After his luncheon and beer he lit his pipe. By this time Buller and Philpotts must have finished their luncheon too, and have started for the stables. They would wonder at first why he did not come, but they would not really care.

And now they must have started. He had done well not to go with them; he would not have enjoyed it, Waters assured himself, repeating the old phrases; he would never enjoy anything again. He looked at his watch furtively. What! they wouldn't start for three minutes yet. Then he had still just time enough to catch them. He seized his hat, and without waiting for a reason—he had no time to wait—he hurried out, Lo-Ben barking at his heels.

# The Claim of the Past

# The Claim of the Past

THEY had all been to luncheon with Mr. Windus, and now, under his guidance, they started out to see the College, walking together across the quadrangle through the summer sunshine. Mr. Windus talked to Mrs. Ellwood of Dalmouth, the Devonshire town where she lived, and he had friends; the others were gossiping of the heat, the Oxford dances, while Ruth Ellwood and young Rutherford came last of all.

Rutherford too belonged to Dalmouth, was, indeed, a cousin of the Ellwoods—all the

Dalmouth families were somehow related; but going away early to school, and afterwards to Oxford, he had come at last to seem more like a stranger to them than a friend or cousin. And this invitation to meet the Ellwoods he had accepted merely out of politeness; he was busy with his work, felt in no mood for the Oxford gaieties, and anyhow cared, or thought he cared, very little indeed for Dalmouth or the Dalmouth people.

But soon he had begun to listen with pleasure and interest to the home news, as his charming cousin told it.

"And so the town isn't much changed?" he asked; "and the different cousins, what has become of them all?"

With eager interest she went on telling him of all the old families, who lived in the different houses; how the young girls had grown up—there were so many pretty ones

## The Claim of the Past

among the cousins!—and the young men had gone into the family offices. Some of them were married and settled down already.

"And Aunt Warner's house under the beeches, with its lawn, where we used to play, is it just the same?"

"Oh, yes, just the same, only the Bartons live there now—Uncle James's family; and on Thursdays we meet there—I mean the cousins' Tennis Club—and when it rains we dance in the old drawing room. But how shocked dear old Aunt Warner would have been to see us!" Then, as they went through the gateway into the College garden, she added, "I'm afraid all this gossip bores you; it's interesting for us who live at home, but for other people—"

"Oh, but I belong to Dalmouth!" he protested.

"Of course you do, only it's so long since

you've been there," she said in half apology, "and we thought—I thought you didn't care."

It was indeed a long time, it was years since he had been there, he remembered with a certain regret for the preoccupation the youthful intolerance, that had made him half despise his home. It was a charming place after all, the grey seaport town with its wharves, and shipping, and narrow streets, and the pleasant homes and gardens just outside where his cousins and uncles, the merchants, lived—where as a boy he had lived. How well he remembered watching, on summer afternoons, the white sails of the family ships, as they floated up with the tide past the green lawns and square old houses. A pleasant life it must be there, he thought, and quite untroubled in its tranquil interests by any great ambitions or ideas—the echoes of which, indeed, could hardly reach them in their quiet old corner of the world.

And, as they talked, the young man began to fancy idly what his own life would have been, had he never gone away from the old Devonshire town. It had been intended, of course, that he should stay there, and take his own part in the family concerns; even yet his uncles were keeping a place for him; and although they feared he was quite spoiled by Oxford, yet they would welcome him back, he knew, should he only give up those ambitions, that to them—and to himself sometimes!—seemed so impossible, so dreamy and unreal.

Ruth Ellwood stopped now and then to look at the garden flowers. "What lovely irises, and how quaint those roses are, trained so stiffly on the old walls."

"Are you fond of gardening?" he asked.

She was very fond of it, she said—not that she knew much about it! But she liked planting things and tying them up, and she always gathered the flowers for the house. Things grew so well at Dalmouth—roses and peonies, and great chrysanthemums in the autumn. Only it made her a little sad to see the chrysanthemums; their summers were so lovely!

Rutherford knew the house in which his cousin lived, and now he could almost see her there, moving over the sweet grass, hatless, in the morning light, to gather roses, filling old china bowls with their fragrant leaves; or walking home on rainy evenings past the great cedar, the wet lawn, and borders of dripping flowers.

"How beautiful she is!" he thought, looking furtively at her. The impression of this beauty, her pleasant voice, the friendly people she spoke of, and all the memories that made them seem so intimate together, affected him with a curious fresh sense of happiness, coming into his life, which had been of late somewhat discouraged and lonely, with a charm as real and actual as that of the warmth of the sun, the scent of roses.

They had reached the end of the garden, and as they turned back, still following the others, he said hesitatingly to his companion something about coming to Dalmouth soon for a visit.

"Oh, do come!" she cried, "I'm sure you'll enjoy it, and they will all be so glad to see you."

"I hope so—but I'm afraid they must think rather badly of me—will be prejudiced against me; you will have to introduce me."

"Oh, I will—only really, they won't be prejudiced against you." Then she added,

"Oxford is so charming!" in a way that touched Rutherford a little. She at least, in spite of all she had heard at home, plainly could see nothing so dreadful or dangerous in Oxford, or her cousin, after all!

Yes, Oxford was charming, she said again, and not at all what she had expected—at first she had been really almost afraid to come! But it was all so pleasant; why had people such a prejudice against the University?—her two brothers wanted to come, but her father would not hear of it. But how could it unfit them for living at home? She had seen how the undergraduates lived. And her brothers would have enjoyed it so. She had been in several of the Colleges now, and had been on the river, and was going out to tea that afternoon, and afterwards, to a dance.

"Tell me," she asked, as they followed the

others towards the chapel door, "are you going to any of the dances?"

He was afraid he wouldn't have the time, he said.

"Oh, what a pity, you ought to come," she cried; but her voice was hushed when, out of the glare and sunshine, they went into the blue obscurity, the cool old smell and quiet of the chapel.

The ladies looked at the windows, the religious carving; and their movement, as they went about, filled with a rustling sound the vacant silence of the place. Then they all gathered in a group while one of the Fellows told them something of the history of the chapel: how it had been built in the fourteenth century, and how ever since then the members of the College had worshipped there, and among them many whose names had afterwards grown famous.

"Tell me," Ruth Ellwood whispered, as they walked away, "is this where the undergraduates sit; where do you sit?" He showed her the Scholars' seats, and the old brass eagle from which they read the lessons, and then, when they went through the ante-chapel, she paused a moment, looking at the inscriptions and monuments.

Were there any nice old epitaphs? she asked. "Do show them to me, if there are."

The rest of the party had left the chapel, but could still be seen through the open door standing not far off in the sunshine, and the gossip of their voices came in faintly now and then.

The old brasses, dating from Gothic times, bore inscriptions in rhyming Latin, that Rutherford read and translated to his companion; there were monuments of a later time, adorned with urns, cherubs, and garlands —old trappings of death that made death itself seem almost quaint and charming. But in the seventeenth century the tranquil records of the scholars' lives were disturbed by echoes of old war and exile. "Reader, look to thy feet! Honest and Loyal men are sleeping under Thee," one inscription ran; and the name of more than one was recorded "who, when Loyalty and the Church fainted, lay down and Died."

Other monuments were put up to the memory of young men who had died at College. Well-born and modest, the old Latin described them, and dead, centuries ago, in the flower of their fruitless years. "Vivere dulce fuit!" one of them had complained, as four hundred years before, in florid Latin, he bade farewell to youth and hope.

Of another it was quaintly said, "Talis erat

vita, qualis stylus, elegans et pura"; while another undergraduate's virtues were recorded in verses ending with the line,

"Expertus praedico, tutor eram."

Then there was an inscription in English verse, from some Cavalier poet, Rutherford thought,

"Him while fresh and fragrant Time
Cherisht in his golden prime;
Ere Hebe's hand had overlaid
His smooth cheeks with downy shade,
The rush of Death's unruly wave
Swept him off into his grave.

. . . . . . .

Eyes are vocall, teares have tongues,
And there be words not made with lungs;
Sententious showres: Oh let them fall!
Their cadence is rhetoricall."

Another of the same date recorded the deeds of the young scholar-soldiers "who, at the news of Battle, changed their Gownes for Armour, and Faithfully served King Charles I.

## The Claim of the Past

from Edge Hill fight, to the End of those unhappie Wars." But one youth in that early conflict had been killed in the pursuit of victory "after Gloriously redeeming, with his own hands, the banner Royal of the King."

So they linger there for a few moments, passing from one to another of the epitaphs, with their records of knightly effort, of the ideal and romantic hopes of youth, completed afterwards, or quenched long ago by early death. And to the young man, as he spells them out, they seem at last to form a continuing tradition of lives dauntlessly lived and lost, and then recorded here, briefly, in this ancient corner of the College. His companion, too, was vaguely charmed and touched by the old inscriptions, and as they turned at last to go out she stopped in front of another tablet. Would he read it? It was too high for her to see.

Rutherford looked at it. "It's a modern one, I don't think it will interest you—"

"Oh yes, it will—do read it."

He looked at it in silence for a minute. Faint sounds of music floated into the dim chapel from the world outside—music, and distant voices calling. Then he read the name and date; a young man who had been drowned the year before. "His companions at School and College have erected this tablet, wishing to preserve the recollection of one who was much beloved, and whose influence for good was greatly felt in this place. He was of a courageous and enthusiastic nature; the example, had he lived, of his generous ambitions—" But in the middle, Rutherford's voice changed a little, and with a shiver his cousin turned and went away. Had she guessed that they had been friends, these two, or was it merely that she felt at last the chill of the place, and of all the old dead about her?

In a moment the young man turns to go out too. But as he looks through the dimness of the chapel on the summer and sunlight, and his cousin standing there outside the door, how far it all seems, how unreal! Only real to him is a sense of the briefness of life, and of the great, difficult things that may nevertheless be done or attempted before death comes. And as he walks away again with his cousin, he is quite certain, now at last, that this is no mere emotion or boyish enthusiasm, but an influence that for evil or good must rule his life—must come, at least, between him and any choice of ease and the common happiness.

*A Broken Journey*

# A Broken Journey

## I.

THE air tasted fresh; through the sunshiny mist the London houses shone beautiful and vague; the passers-by seemed to be whistling and singing as they went to their morning work. Already at Paddington cabs were arriving; they drove down under the clock in an endless procession; the family luggage was unloaded, and the passengers, muffled for winter journeys, hurried into the station.

Then a hansom pulled up sharply, and a

young man got out, whose air of fashion and slim figure, as he stood there paying his driver, drew for a moment the notice of the other travellers.

On the platform within, by the waiting trains, all was movement; the great adventurous station was full of grey light, and a confusion of sounds and echoes. Arthur Lestrange, as he walked across, looked about with quick eyes on the orderly tumult, the heaps of moving luggage, the hurrying people. They were all starting off on pleasant holiday journeys, he fancied; indeed, everything seemed eager and gay that morning.

He chose an empty first-class carriage in the train going northwards; but in a moment he hurried out back to the bookstall to get a paper, and returned with several novels in his hands. On the top of one was pictured, in bright tragic colours, a young

## A Broken Journey

man suspended over the edge of a perilous cliff.

"Why did I buy them?" Arthur wondered, looking at the books with amusement.

Settling himself again, he watched through his window the anxious procession of people who came peering by, looking for corner seats. Then he saw his own luggage passing.

"Oh, you can put those things in here with me," he called out to the porter.

"I've labelled them, sir," the porter said, looking up with a stupid face.

"Put them in, put them in, don't you see there's plenty of room," Arthur said with a certain sharpness and nervous agitation.

There were two young men standing on the platform near his window.

"Well, good-bye," one of them said, as he looked at the other with friendly eyes, "you mustn't wait, and you'll come up and see us, won't you?"

They were Oxford men, young Lestrange thought, as he watched them, feeling envious, and almost lonely for a moment as he remembered the times when he had travelled down so often with friends from Paddington to Oxford.

But surely it was time for the train to start! The movement on the platform seemed to be increasing; the tumult and screaming whistles sounded louder and louder in his ears, as he waited, leaning uncomfortably forward.

At last all the doors were shut; the platform grew more vacant; a few belated people hurried up; a green flag was waved; a whistle blown; everything about him seemed to glide backwards, and then, with the shaking and noise of travel, the train drew itself slowly out of the station. Arthur leaned back

## A Broken Journey

with a sensation of immense relief. He was really away at last. Away from everybody! He had been almost afraid that they might come to the station and try to stop him. But it was absurd, he told himself, as he opened the morning paper, it was absurd to make so much trouble; for what was there to bother about? He could take care of himself; and anyhow his relations had better mind their own business. As for talking about ruin! He thought of his pompous uncle and dull pale cousins, and then of the people with whom he was going to stay.

"Good old ruin," he said half aloud, running down the news of the day with eyes that hardly noticed what he read. In a moment he turned to look out of the window.

After making its way through the suburbs, the train had begun at last to travel more quickly through the open country. The trees and earth and houses near at hand drifted backwards; the more distant fields moved back with a slower motion, while the horizon seemed to glide forward with the train. The sun shone on the brown earth and mist and leafless trees; a young horse galloped the length of his field in a playful race with the moving carriages.

Young Lestrange changed his seat restlessly. Then he began to rearrange his luggage on the rack; he looked at himself in the mirror, caressing his slight moustache. His hair was smooth and dark over his handsome young face. Only his straight eyebrows, twitching nervously now and then, would give him rather a harassed, anxious look for a moment.

What was the use of bothering, he said to himself, smiling as he turned carelessly away. If one was young! Men sowed their wild oats; he would settle down soon enough, but in the meantime he would enjoy himself. You have only one life to live. . . .

The winter morning seemed unusually bright and clear; the train went swiftly; its wheels beat on the rails an unquiet and delicious measure, answering and echoing his thoughts. Restless and excited, he again threw down the paper, for the bright images of desire, that floated before his eyes, made the printed words seem almost meaningless.

He pictured to himself the end of his journey—the trap that would probably meet him—a dog-cart, with shining bay horse and man in livery, standing in the gravel sweep of a country station. The drive up, and then at tea, or just before dinner, he and she would meet in the drawing room, greeting each other with pretended indifference. How he hated and loved her!

## A Broken Journey

After a while the train, going more slowly now, began to draw into Reading. With the beginnings of weariness and headache Arthur looked at the waste of railway trucks, the heaps of coal and blackened snow, the red factory buildings, and the dreary streets beyond. Biscuit factories—who could eat all the biscuits they made? he wondered; "Clapper's Restaurant"—suppose you should dine there, they would give you nothing but biscuits, probably. Did the train stop at Reading?—he could get some spirits at the refreshment room.

At the bar, Lestrange saw the figure and long grey coat of a man he thought he recognized; and then, getting sight of Boyle's smooth-shaven face, and remembering his supercilious manners and reputation, he felt with sudden repulsion how much he hated men of that kind—men of pleasure, who were no longer young. When you were young it was different—but to go on always. . . .

But when Boyle turned and greeted him in an indifferent, half-friendly way, and then walked up and down with him on the platform, Arthur could not help feeling, in spite of himself, somewhat flattered and pleased. After all, Boyle knew most of the best people, and went everywhere.

"I have an empty carriage; you might as well come in with me, if you are by yourself." Boyle seemed not unwilling, and soon appeared at Arthur's carriage.

"I'm just on my way to Marcham," Arthur said, as if casually; "the Vallences', you know." There was a slight lisp in his pleasant musical voice.

Boyle was putting his golf clubs in the rack, but turned round at this and glanced at Arthur oddly. However he said nothing, and after a moment he sat down, and, lighting a cigarette, began looking at the paper.

As the train went out of Reading they began to talk, or rather Arthur talked. Soon he was discussing horses and actresses and gambling debts. It was a good game, baccarat, Arthur said, but you had to pay for it sometimes. He had just dropped a cool thousand or two, which was rather a bore. There was a music hall singer to whom Arthur referred more than once as "Mamie."

"And how about Lulu, hey?" Boyle asked, with his disagreeable laugh.

"Oh, Lulu—good old Lulu!" Arthur said, but he really had no idea of what Boyle meant.

Boyle told a story in his short, indifferent way, and Arthur exclaimed, "Capital! capital!" and laughed loudly in the fashion of a popular man he knew.

Had he ever been to the Vallences' before? Boyle asked.

No, he had never gone before. Did Boyle know them?—Boyle had been there; was going there now, in fact, he said.

"Really, are you going there now? How odd we should meet like this!" They talked a little about the place and people. It would be rather a lively set, wouldn't it? Arthur asked; and he boasted that his uncle, Lord Seabury, had warned him against them. But, good God! what did he care if people were amusing. "Do you know who else will be there?"

"Oh, a lot of people. Mrs. Stair (Arthur blushed at this), and that young Glass."

"Glass?" Arthur exclaimed; "oh, not really that man! They can't like him."

"They like his money."

"You don't mean they ask a man—a stupid boy like that—to get his money."

"They don't say they do," and Boyle looked up from his paper with an expression that seemed to say, "You young fool, you don't know much."

("Is that what I'm asked for?" Arthur wondered for a second.)

"I say, did you read about that young Hughes?" Boyle was saying. "It seems he's gone and played the fool—shot himself; wrote to his mamma he was ruined. So he won't be there."

"Used he to go to Marcham?"

"Oh, always there."

"Well, it's the pace that kills," Arthur said sententiously, though his hand, as he lighted another cigarette, shook a little. "It isn't everyone that can stand the racket."

"If they weren't all such sickening young

fools," Boyle replied in a short contemptuous way, as if the talk bored him.

" He thinks a damned lot of himself," Arthur thought, looking with a sidelong glance at Boyle. His head began to ache again; a sudden disgust came over him; he felt he hated Boyle. And he hated himself too, for talking and boasting as he had talked and boasted but a few minutes before. And they were all like Boyle, all those people; they cared only for his name and money. "Name and money, name and money," the wheels beat on the rails. Well, soon he would lose them, most likely—his name and money— like the young suicide, who had lost them both and his life too.

Still he made an effort to ward off the mood that was settling down on him—the mood he knew so well! He was not ruined, he told himself, and there was nothing ruinous in an ordinary visit. He could take care of himself. The chief of his debts were gambling debts, and he was going to stop playing soon; would settle down quietly; he would make a resolution, and keep to it.

But what was he doing now in that rattling train? Only the day before he had resolved not to come; had promised solemnly that he would not come; had made a resolution to break with all that set, and not yield to the passion which people said would ruin him. Yet here he was, going on to it all! There seemed to him something sinister in his journey, something fatal in the swiftness of the rattling train, as if he were being carried on to a dreadful place, and into misfortune, against his will. He leaned away from Boyle, and touched his cheek to the cool pane of the window. Masses of steam enveloped the train, but Arthur saw the quiet landscape now and then, glimpses of faded green fields with snow, and, over the hedges, the shining river, and bluish hills beyond. He saw a boat on the river; recognized a bit of wood, a church tower. Those were the hills that he had ridden over; the lanes through which he had so often walked; the river down which he had floated in the summer sunshine, pulling up refreshed and strong after bathing. With an eager, almost childish interest he waited for the green visions, through the shifting steam, of these familiar places.

He opened the window; the singing air tasted pleasantly cool and fresh. Over the flooded fields and the moving trees he saw the spires and towers of Oxford. He could well remember the quiet streets there; seemed to see himself, indeed, moving through them; and he almost believed that in a few minutes he would be driving up, as he had driven up so often before, in that procession of racing cabs to the old College, and to all his friends.

The steam blew again about the train, wrapped his face in its warm breath, and blotted out the view. Inside the shaking carriage was the tobacco smoke, and his luggage. "Where am I going with that man?" he asked himself suddenly, for the picture of Oxford had filled his mind entirely for a moment. The buildings and towers were so near now, the water of the reservoir gleamed slowly past. Arthur took down his luggage from the rack. At the bottom of his mind he had been wanting for a long time to go back to Oxford, and see it all, and see an old friend there; and so, eagerly, almost before the train had stopped, he hailed a porter and got out of the carriage.

## A Broken Journey

"I must stay over here a few hours," he said to Boyle, with apparent calmness. "There is something I have just thought of, and must attend to. I'll telegraph, but you'd better tell them, though, not to meet me." He turned and walked away.

But as he drove up to Oxford, "What a fool I am," he kept saying to himself. Indeed Boyle's surprise, the commonplace platform, the ticket-collector's questions, the sight outside of his own luggage being lifted up on a hansom, had soon made his foolish, helpless impulse fade, like the flame of a candle, taken out into the daylight and windy air. But to go back to the train would have seemed doubly foolish, so, borne on by the impetus of his dead desire, he drove away. The next train was not till half-past six. He would get luncheon, and, after all, it might be pleasant to see the old place. But he was resolved that never again would he act on those stupid, sudden ideas—they made him seem like a fool.

II.

After luncheon Arthur went out—the time had to be spent somehow—and walked idly along the High Street. It was all so familiar: the shops, the windows of the club to which he had belonged, the rooms where his friends had lived. But he knew no one now. The streets were wet with winter mud, there was a commonplace light on the houses, and Arthur looked about him with very little interest and emotion. Walking past the Colleges, he loitered for a little on Magdalen Bridge, and then turned back again. It was still early, and he began to meet now the young men who were starting out of Oxford for the open air and country. Some were dressed for football; three or four in brown coats rode by on horses, talking and laughing as they passed; but the greater number were in flannels, and moving towards the river. These Arthur followed—he had nothing else to do—through the streets and meadows, coming at last to the barges and windy river. Men were calling to each other, boats were pushing out, and the turbid current of the Thames ran swiftly with the winter floods.

But for him there was too much sound about the wind and water, the cold sunshine was too bright and harsh, and he felt doubly weary, as he looked at all that life and activity and health. And yet once he would have delighted in it.

When Arthur Lestrange had come first from school to Oxford, he had entered with eagerness and youthful ambition into the pleasures and activities of university life, wishing to do everything well that he tried to do, and with distinction if he could. And all these ambitions and activities he came to share, in the pleasant, intimate Oxford way, with a friend, slightly older than himself.

But after a while he began to grow discontented; success was not so easy;—and what was the good of it after all? he asked himself, with impatient lassitude. Finding new friends and more exciting pleasures, he gradually drifted away from his old companions. What was the harm? he said impatiently to Austen, resenting his friend's affectionate advice. He would enjoy life as other people enjoyed it; he only wanted to be left alone. So they grew less intimate; and when Lestrange found himself in trouble, serious enough to make him leave Oxford, he had been too angry and proud to see Austen, or answer his friendly letter. "How stupid it has all been," he said to himself, the memory of all this coming over him rather drearily, as he walked back towards Oxford.

But his feeble attempts to make some change in his life—these were the stupidest of all his memories; how, when his father died abroad, he was really frightened, fearing for himself a death like that, and going back to the half-neglected place that was now his own, he remembered his old plans of life, and tried to do his duty there, and be a good landlord and neighbour. But in a few months he grew weary of it all; it was too lonely, too depressing. . . .

And then a year after, when he hoped for a while that a nice girl he knew might care for him; and this last time, when his losses at play had made him mortgage his property still more heavily. Then, sobered for a moment by his uncle's warnings, and by the ruin that seemed not far off, he suddenly resolved to change, to give up playing, to keep away from all those people.

But he had started for Marcham after all. It was no good trying, and no one cared. Of course no one cared—why should they? With worldly derision he remembered now the foolish, tattered hope he had cherished all along—the hope that some day, coming back to Oxford, he would find the old life, the old friend, who *had* cared once. And without stopping he walked past his College, the place where Austen was still living. He did not want to see any of them, nor would they want to see him.

Oppressed by the slowness of the time, the afternoon quiet of the streets, he resolved to go back to the station and wait there, watching the railway clock slowly eat up the hours. But passing by chance the livery stable where he had always kept his horses, with an aimless impulse he sauntered into the open court. One of the stable grooms coming up, addressed him by name, and asked him if he wanted to order a horse.

"It's a long while since we've seen you in Oxford, sir."

This recognition and friendly look in the man's face, touched Arthur, and, with a revival of eagerness, he felt that a ride would be just the thing to kill the time. So, ordering a horse to be sent to the hotel where he had left his luggage, he hurried back to get ready.

### III.

As he rode back towards Oxford, two hours afterwards, the light was already fading from the winter sky. Sleepily and quietly he jogged along now, his horse tired at last after the quick gallop through grass lanes and over the wet fields and commons. The young man, too, was tired; but with a healthy, physical fatigue, pleasant in all his body. He felt almost happy after the motion, the wide light, the freshness of the air. And when he rode into the old city, walking his horse through the darkening streets, it seemed to him as if he were riding home now, as often he had ridden home into Oxford before, at just this hour of the twilight. The groups in the doorways, the lighted windows in the dim buildings, the sounds about him of bells and footsteps and friendly voices, brought back to him confusedly, mixed with the memory of this and that, the charm and comfort of that old life—that life of order and disciplined ways, and high old-fashioned purposes. How quietly the days had gone by: the mornings of work, the rides with friends, or afternoons on the river, between the yellowing autumn willows; the evenings with the white lamp-light and pleasant talk and books. He had quarrelled with the restraint, the subordination, sometimes; had thought it too severe, too painful, to go out on the river in the wind and rain, to get up so early in the cold of winter mornings. But now, after the stale dissipation of his life, it was only the friendly warmth, the lazily-wasted hours he remembered, the pleasant fatigue after exercise, and the taste of the winter air when he had hurried out to chapel through the earliest sunlight.

If he could only go back to it all; if,

putting up his horse, he could walk to his rooms through the twilight, and find his books, and the fire burning there, and friends not far off! But things had been against him somehow. And yet he had meant it all to be so different. And with half a sigh he remembered the summer evenings when he and Austen had walked in the old garden, talking of their plans in life—of all they meant to do—together! if they could. But then, people never did remain friends like that.

When he gave up his horse, however, he looked at his watch, and, after standing in hesitation for a moment, he turned with a sudden impulse, and walked quickly towards his old College.

In the porch stood a group of undergraduates, just up from the river, and vaguely gossiping before they separated. But they were all strangers to Arthur, and the porter, who answered his questions, was a stranger too. Crossing the darker quadrangle, the young man went into a staircase and up two flights of steps. Then he stopped, and stood breathing quickly for a moment. There was the door, and the name over it, but he had grown suddenly ashamed of his errand. Austen might have forgotten him, or might not want to see him. . . . But, bah! what did he care? and his footsteps must have been heard. . . .

"I'm afraid you don't recognize me," Arthur said, in his assured voice, as he went forward into the room. "I was in Oxford; I thought I'd look you up."

Austen, who was sitting by a lamp, turned round with a puzzled expression on his staid, pleasant face. Then, pushing aside a heap of papers, he got up and said: "Oh, Lestrange, I didn't recognize you at first, it's so dark there. But I'm glad to see you—do sit down; you'll have tea, won't you?"

He was passing through Oxford, Arthur said; and having a few hours on his hands after riding over Shotover, he had come back, and happened to look in at the old College. The plausibility of this explanation, and Austen's voice as he said politely, "That's right, that's right, I'm delighted to see you again," soon overcame most of the shyness behind Arthur's easy, unembarrassed manner. They still talked to each other rather formally, however, as men do who have not met for years.

"It's a long time since you've been in Oxford, isn't it?" Austen asked.

"Yes, it is; I've been at home, in London. But I suppose it hasn't changed much."

No, there wasn't much change, Austen said; old people went and new came.

What had become of all the men who had been with them in College, Arthur asked; he had lost sight of them somehow.

Austen said that some were at the Bar; some in the government offices; one or two in Parliament already; the most of them seemed to be getting on pretty well, he thought, though he had lost sight of many of them, as one did.

"And you've been living on here ever since? I heard you had been made a Fellow. You like it, I suppose?"

Yes, Austen said, he liked it well enough, the work was tiring sometimes; that afternoon he had been going through papers. Arthur noticed that he looked fatigued, and a good deal older. It was dry, hard work no doubt, but still it was not the kind of thing that changed you.

"I say, you have jolly rooms here, Austen; I envy you living in a place like this. Do you remember your old rooms over the garden? I think I used to live in them almost."

As the old memories revived they seemed to grow less shy of each other. Arthur leaned forward, talking in a vague, intermittent way as he stared into the fire. Sometimes he would gaze at nothing, with a vacant, dazed look, for minutes together; or he would take the fire-irons and break up the coals. Once the tongs slipped and fell with a sudden clatter; he started nervously.

"Well," he said at last, rousing himself from a reverie in which he seemed conscious of nothing but the warmth and comfort and pleasant, physical fatigue, "Well, it seems very jolly here, like old times; I almost wish I had never gone away. But then, of course,

I couldn't help it," he added; "I wasn't asked."

"You had hard luck," Austen said; "I hope it hasn't made any difference."

The words sounded friendly and sympathetic to Arthur. Hard luck, yes, that was it; he had always had hard luck.

"What have you been doing since?" Austen said politely.

"What have I been doing, Charles? Oh, nothing much; seeing about things at home a little. There were some cottages I had rebuilt. You remember we used to talk about it. It isn't so easy though, or I suppose I'm not so clever at it. But of course you know a great deal more about those things."

"No, oh no! I've been so busy. That sort of thing is good in moderation, and I'm glad you keep it up."

"Oh yes, in a way . . . but no, what am I saying? I don't really keep it up. It was all two years ago. I haven't done much of anything since—anything good. Things, you know," he went on, as he stared into the fire, "haven't gone just—I mean, it's been rather stupid—stupid, and worse, I'm afraid; I don't seem good for much somehow."

The familiar Oxford room, with its order, and books, and shaded light, seemed so shut in, so far from the friendless world in which he lived, that for the moment Arthur almost forgot the lonely distrust, the derision of everything, which his life had taught him. "I suppose it's fate," he added, staring into the fire, as if he were half-ashamed of what he was saying. "I suppose it *is* fate—but still, I wonder—sometimes it seems if—that if I had had a chance, if anybody—" He waited a minute indecisively. But Austen said nothing. Arthur glanced at him, and then, flushing slightly, he got up. "But I must be going now," he said, with a curious change and coldness in his voice; "I have a train to catch."

"Oh, don't go," Austen replied awkwardly, "don't go just yet. I'm sorry to hear what you say; but don't you think, if you will allow me to say so, don't you think it is a mistake to blame fate for such things? If you would tell me more—"

"Oh, thanks," Arthur said, "I think I must be going."

"But you were going to say something," Austen urged, "and if you would tell me more, I might be able to help you, or give you advice at least."

Arthur glanced at him quickly. Then suddenly the idea seemed to amuse him, and coming back a step or two he said, with a smile, "Tell you more, Austen? Oh, I was only going to tell you what everyone knows, that I've turned out a bad lot, that's all."

"I'm sorry to hear that," said Austen, in a rather shocked voice; "I hope it's not so bad."

Arthur smiled pleasantly. "Oh well, you know, it *is* pretty bad, I'm afraid."

"But what do you mean, Lestrange?"

"What do I mean? Oh, all the usual things—bad company, gambling, and women."

Austen looked still more shocked. "But surely you could change if you wanted to!"

"I suppose I might, if I wanted to," Arthur said, playing with his riding whip. "But I'm afraid I don't want to. What's the good?"

"What's the good?" Austen repeated. "I don't see how you can ask such a question; if what you say is true, you ought to want to change."

Arthur mused a moment. Then looking up, with apparent candour, he said, "Well, I suppose it is odd; but honestly, you know, I don't want to change in the least. You see, your respectable people, they don't want to have anything to do with me; and anyhow, the things they care for bore me to death, really they do. You only have one life, so why not be happy in your own way? that's my principle."

"But surely, Lestrange, you can't go on—"

"No, I suppose I can't for ever; but you try to enjoy it while it lasts; and anyhow, my father, you know how he died—I suppose it's fate; heredity you call those things, don't you?"

"Really, I'm shocked to hear you talk so recklessly, as if you didn't care. You seem very much changed."

"Am I changed? I don't know; I suppose

I am. We've both changed a little, don't you think? At least, things seem different. I wonder where I put my gloves,—I really must be going."

"Well, of course, I can't keep you, Lestrange; I can only give you my advice. But I can't believe you're happy."

For a moment Arthur looked at him sullenly.

"Well, what if I ain't?" he asked. "What's that to you?"

"I was only going to say," Austen went on, "I was only going to say that it seems to me that if you would try—"

"Try! Good Lord, I've tried enough, but what's the good?" Arthur said, with his old calmness and indifference, as he turned away towards the door. "I don't care, and no one else does, either. But I must be off. Good bye."

# A Broken Journey

He went down the steps quickly, whistling as he walked away through the darkness. He was angry at himself, and bitterly ashamed of his visit to Austen. They were all like that—he ought to have known. And yet it was a pity, too!

# The Sub-Warden

# The Sub-Warden

THE two old gentlemen walked out of the Common Room, across the quadrangle to the porter's lodge: the Vicar of North Mims, who had been spending a few hours in Oxford and dining in College, wanted to catch the evening train back to North Mims, the College living he had held for the last ten years, and the Sub-Warden wanted to see the last of him.

"The point I make is this," the old Vicar said again, frowning with his bushy eyebrows in the moonlight; "the point I make is this:

## The Sub-Warden

There would be no trouble at all, if it wasn't for the drinking. If they want meetings, let them have Temperance meetings; and I say that those Socialist fellows from London have absolutely no business meddling in the affairs of my parish. And as for the undergraduates who come out from Oxford to speak"—the Vicar's voice grew more solemnly irate—"as for those undergraduates, they should be punished. It is, I consider, a case in which both college and university authorities should intervene with prompt severity."

They walked on for a little in silence, and then the Sub-Warden said, as he looked at his companion, "Really, Philpotts, you know, you ought to tricycle."

The truth is, that, as they had sat in the Common Room over their port, the Rev. Mr. Philpotts had repeated himself a great many times; and, the Sub-Warden's mind at

## The Sub-Warden

last beginning to wander, he had said to himself, as he looked at his glass and then at his old friend, "Really, Philpotts is getting very heavy! I used to be heavier, and probably should be now, if it wasn't for tricycling!" And, his mind being full of the thought, he had suddenly said, "Really, Philpotts, you know, you ought to tricycle!"

"What!" said the Vicar, in a voice of slow amazement. "What on earth has tricycling got to do with it?"

"Oh, I beg your pardon!" the Sub-Warden cried, who was the soul of good-nature, "I am so absent-minded. You were speaking of the Radicals; it is certainly shocking."

"Radicals! Pestilent Socialists I call them," and the Vicar's mind, after its jolt, got back into the old groove. "Why, you would hardly believe it, but they had the impertinence to advertise some young ninny as a member of this College, and they actually posted it on the vicarage gate. My wife had to soak it off with a sponge. Now, what I say is—"

But they had arrived in the porch, and the Sub-Warden, telling the Vicar it was late, hurried him out of College, and then turned and walked back to his rooms.

"He certainly is getting heavy," he said to himself. "He has changed very much. These country livings! And if I had only started to ride a little earlier this afternoon, he wouldn't have caught me. Another time when I miss my exercise I mustn't drink port! At my age one begins to feel it."

The Sub-Warden reached his staircase, and, resting one hand on the wall of the building, he turned and looked at the moon. Then he went upstairs, but, instead of sitting down at his table, he went to the window and

## The Sub-Warden

opened the sash. There was a curious look about the trees and buildings, as if they had been turning round, and had just stopped. It was odd. Poor old Philpotts! What an undergraduate he had been—up to anything! What times they had had! And now he was on his way back to his wife at North Mims! The Sub-Warden sighed; then smiled, and, straightening himself, after a moment's hesitation, he went and put on an old coat, and stole with soft steps out of the College. Perhaps it was the moonlight; perhaps an old memory or two that had come back to him, or the thought of the exercise he had missed; or, again (but this is mere conjecture), the glass or two of College port may have done something to put his mind in a mood for adventure. Anyhow, he got on his tricycle, and started for a ride into the country. He only hoped the Bursar had not seen him; not that there was any reason why he shouldn't ride at night, but the Bursar made up such funny stories about the Sub-Warden and his tricycle rides.

And so he rode lightly along, over the vague roads, barred here and there by the blue shadows of the trees—rode lightly along through the ancient Oxfordshire country; and he laughed in his genial Tory heart as he thought of the Vicar's absurd political panic. No, a ripple of Radical excitement in the towns perhaps, but it would hardly touch the country. The labourers must know who were their real friends and leaders. And yet it was outrageous, he thought, as he began pushing his machine up a hill, it was outrageous that anyone should have such views. But that members of the University should go and speak at their dreadful meetings! The Sub-Warden shook his head and

## The Sub-Warden

sighed, as he thought of the University—its sad change, its evil state. Could it, indeed, be still called a University? Ah, in the old days, before the Royal Commissions! But when he mounted his machine again at the top of the hill, he forgot these black thoughts, and rode quickly down—indeed, he almost felt himself on wings—into the village he saw below him, an old village, spread out asleep in the moonlight. He went on slow wheels through the blue-shadowed streets; he breathed in the night air, sweet-scented from the village gardens; he felt young in his soul, and would hardly recognize as his own the respectable, fat shadow that wheeled after him across each moonlit space.

All at once, in the midst of the sleeping village, there appeared in front of him a square red building, with brightly lighted windows. Curious to know what was going on, he rode his machine up to one of the windows, and, looking through the glass, misty from the heat and perspiration within, he saw vague rows of dark figures, and an upright shape moving its arms at the end of the hall. What could it be? Around at the door, whither he wheeled himself, there was a big poster, partly torn, with the word "Temperance" on it, and something else pinned across it. "That's right, that's right!" the Sub-Warden exclaimed, "that's the way to cut the ground from under the Radicals! Philpotts was right; it's a question of drink, not of politics."

And so he got down from his tricycle and went in for a moment. Dazed by the heat and light, he stood still and stared about. The orator also stopped and stared at him. There were bright texts of Scripture and temperance mottoes on the walls; but the Sub-Warden kept gazing at these words, "The

Lord is at Hand," hung in large letters over the orator's head. But this orator was Thomas Woolley, his own pupil! Soon it all seemed clear to him. Woolley was known as a Temperance speaker, and here he had come to hold a meeting in a little village. The Sub-Warden applauded, and Woolley began to speak again. But as he gasped a good deal, and stuttered, the Sub-Warden could only catch phrases here and there—cold remnants, they seemed to be, of what must have been written as a fiery peroration. "The down-trodden—I mean the inactive . . . the great heart of humanity—and—and—things—. . . . Now is the time for hand to join in hand, and rush to the banner—I mean, it would be better if you would sign your names."

("That's the pledge-book," the Sub-Warden thought. "Yes, I dare say it's right; you could not preach moderate drinking to labourers.")

## The Sub-Warden

"Deliver yourself from the classes—that—that profit by your weakness. . . ."

("That's the public-house keepers," the Sub-Warden reflected. "But why does he call them classes?")

Woolley stared hard at the notes which he gripped in his hand, and then he turned and pointed at a place at the back of the platform, which he called "the Future," and began to speak about a model dwelling, a cow, and a vine and fig-tree; then his voice sank, and he wavered and sat down.

"He expects a good deal from Temperance," the Sub-Warden thought; "what a thing it is to be young!" And he applauded with vigour, such vigour that several rustics in the audience turned and fixed him with their ruminating eyes. Then the Sub-Warden rose (he never spoke in public, but as he had interrupted this meeting!), rose with dignity and internal

## The Sub-Warden

tremors, and made a few smiling remarks; nothing very definite, for, after all, he was not a total abstainer; just his sympathy with the speech of his young friend, his entire approval of the objects of the meeting, his regret that academic duties held him back from a more active participation in the work. . . . But if there was anything that he or the College authorities could do to forward the cause—he believed that their College owned land in the neighbourhood—they must not hesitate to call upon him. Then a mild joke, and he sat down and wiped his face.

Certainly his speech was a great success. Woolley stared wildly at him, but the audience applauded with vigour, and, as they were giving three cheers for "the old College gentleman," the Sub-Warden slipped modestly out. It was hot in there, and they might be handing pledge-books about.

## The Sub-Warden

The mood in which he rode home was a pleasant one. Really he had never heard applause that was quite so warm, so evidently sincere, so spontaneous. There had been nothing like it when the Warden of St. Mary's had spoken at the Corn Exchange. And Temperance was such a dull subject! It was a bore, of course, for a man who loved his quiet to find he had the power of moving an audience; but still, if the Radicals were working so hard, the other side must come forward.

The Sub-Warden went back into College, and, as he was walking across the quadrangle, he heard a tumult of cheers and cries burst out on the moon-lit stillness of the night. He started—the sounds fitted in so well with his dreams! But, of course, it was a Debating Society; and the window being open, the Sub-Warden went up and listened in his new quality of an amateur. A small young man, with a round face and deep voice, was thumping on a table. "What is the meaning, the outcome of this agitation? It is putting blood into the mouth of a tiger"—(applause)—"and when once the tiger has tasted blood, has tasted property that is not his own, it demands more, and it will have it! Yes, sir," he said, turning with a fierce look at the good-natured president of the society, "mark my words, when the poor have divided, like the tiger, everything there is to be divided; when there is nothing left to feed their rage, then, sir, they will turn and rend themselves—like the tiger!"

Great shouts of applause roared through the window, and the bald-headed old gentleman listening outside smiled an indulgent smile. But as the speaker went on, denouncing more definitely the Radical agitators, and even Woolley, by name, the smile faded from the Sub-Warden's face. It must have been a Temperance meeting; and yet—and yet—"Temperance" had been printed on the poster—but hadn't there been something pinned over that, something which he hadn't read? The Sub-Warden looked about. He could see one or two towers against the faint sky, and near each College tower was a Common Room, and in each Common Room the Fellows sat after dinner, telling stories. But suppose he had really spoken at a meeting which—which wasn't a Temperance meeting, and the Bursar should hear of it!

The Sub-Warden lurked about in the quadrangle, holding his hat in his hand, and spying out for Woolley. He came at last.

"Good evening, Woolley," he said, "you have come from the Temperance meeting?"

## The Sub-Warden

"Oh, sir, it wasn't a Temperance meeting, that was the night before!"

"Oh!" said the Sub-Warden, coldly.

"No, sir, it was a different meeting; in fact, the Radical League. I was so afraid—"

"What! Then it was very wrong of you, Woolley, to give me to understand it was a Temperance meeting."

"Oh, please, sir—"

"Don't try to explain it, it admits of no explanation," the Sub-Warden said severely. "I should be sorry to get you into trouble, Woolley, but if this should get to be known, I couldn't answer for the consequences. I shall take no steps personally to make it known, and I should advise you to mention it to no one—to no one at all, do you understand? It's—it's nothing to be proud of."

He walked indignantly away; and, indeed, for the moment his words had made him feel really indignant. But when, on turning a corner, he glanced back and saw the honest Woolley still standing there, he hesitated. Should he return and explain? He took a step back, then he thought of the Bursar, and, with a sudden, sinking fear he went quickly to his room.

*Idyll*

# Idyll

### I.

"I WISH they hadn't asked me," said Matthew Craik, the Logic tutor of St. Mary's, as he looked down at the party in the old secluded College garden. "I wonder," he added, glancing at the reflection of his red tie in the glass, his new tie, his black coat, his young and scholarly face, "I wonder —but no, it isn't too red; they wear them red," he continued, with attempted cheerfulness. "No—," but hearing the laughter of ladies below his window, he scuttled back hastily.

# Idyll

His rooms were high up in the garden tower, almost up amongst the topmost boughs of the College elms; and when, after a moment, he returned to his window and peered down, he could see, through the green of the trees, the white and pink of ladies' dresses, dappling the lawn, and moving and meeting on the College paths. Among the summer leaves the summer wind was breathing; now and then it blew in at the window, laden with scents from the garden, and the happy stir and hum of human voices; and Matthew Craik, or the Corn-Craik, as the undergraduates called him, felt his heart beating high with an unwonted emotion of youth and excitement.

The early philosophers of Asia Minor were very remarkable and suggestive men; but they had lived a long while ago, and now that he had finished and published his book about them, he meant to enjoy himself a little. And what shallow wisdom it was, moreover, to live in the almost solitary way he had been living all the winter. All the winter! All his life really; wasting his youth among books, and almost shut out from everything that is light and amiable in experience. Why, the greenest of his undergraduate pupils might easily know more of modern life than he did.

"Oh, don't harp so on modern life!" his friend Ranken, the junior Dean of St. Thomas', often said to him in his acrid way. "Do for pity's sake leave it alone and stick to your Asia Minor."

But then Ranken was absurdly cynical. Craik recalled with amusement some of the remarks he had made during the winter, when they walked out together for their Sunday walks; remembering how, as they returned in

## Idyll

the dusk through the red fringe of villas between Oxford and the country, Ranken had sometimes paused opposite an uncurtained window, and made merry, with bitter merriment, over the domestic picture they saw in the golden light within,—a family at tea very likely, or an academic parent romping with his children. Craik had always listened in uncontradicting silence; only, standing in the chill gray of the twilight, he would draw his coat about him more tightly; and afterwards, alone in his rooms, these visions would sometimes haunt him, and not unpleasantly.

As he looked down now, it was agreeable to him to see so many ladies in the old garden; he had never quite believed that Ranken had very authentic grounds for his narrow prejudice. For Ranken would have liked to shut ladies out of Oxford altogether; and would have liked to keep it a tranquil home of learning and celibacy, as it used to be before the Royal Commission had granted the Fellows the liberty of marrying. For this unblest liberty, he maintained, had filled the University with frivolity and ladies, and so destroyed the old character of the place that now, as was notorious, the whole of the Summer Term, with a good part of the rest of the academic year, was given over to dances, and picnics, and parties, and other silly and deteriorating trifles. Craik had not been able to contradict his friend, for hitherto the sounds and echoes of this social dissipation had hardly reached his retired corner, save as he had heard them reverberating through the gloomy caverns of Ranken's imagination. But he could not quite believe— here Craik began to laugh, for his eye at that moment was caught by the gargoyle just above him, which was also leaning over and looking into the sunshiny garden. For hundreds of years it had sat there making faces, but now its visage seemed more than ever twisted with a look of Gothic cynicism. As Craik lingered, looking out, himself almost like a second gargoyle, he thought he could see in the garden below two ladies of his acquaintance, Mrs. Cotton and Mrs. Trotter. How ridiculous Ranken was in his views! almost as grotesque as the gargoyle. Craik took his hat and stick, and started downstairs. He would see for himself.

II.

It was very worldly and very brilliant in the garden. Beside a crowd of ladies and young men, three Professors and two Heads of Houses had already arrived, and others were expected.

# Idyll

Mr. White, Mr. Long, and Mr. Maple Fetters, the young unmarried Fellows who were giving the party, kept glancing toward the gateway, over the shoulders of their arriving guests—all smiles, however, as they greeted their friends with apposite remarks. On tables under the trees white cloths were spread, looking almost blue in the vivid green, and on them were plates of red strawberries, ancient silver bowls of sugar, and dewy jugs of lemonade. Sounds of discreet gaiety, voices and laughter, and the tinkling of glasses, quickened the sleepy silence of the garden; while from beneath a high and fleecy cloud the rays of the westering sun brightened the tree-tops and walls, lingered on the ladies' dresses, and streaked with blue shadows the old green lawn. It put Craik in mind of old coloured French pictures he had seen, or the courtly fêtes he had read of; he thought, too, of the garden party in "*Love's Cottage*," a pretty novel he had looked at lately, the party where Miss Molyneux first meets Pastorel the poet.

He kept smiling as he moved about, but he really felt rather shy and alien; if he only knew more people, and could be seen laughing and talking and moving his hands, like the other young men!

He came across one of his pupils at last, and began to speak to him of the recent boat-races in an animated way. But the undergraduate moved off suddenly, with a hasty excuse, to join some ladies who had just arrived, and Craik heard himself observing to a bush that "Brazenose had rowed very well." The observation, he felt, was not brilliant, even for conversation with a freshman; but as a fragment of soliloquy! He looked round; no one could have overheard him? Soon he met his friend, Mrs. Cotton, the wife of Professor Cotton, and he begged to be allowed to get her an ice, or some other refreshment. The pink ice and biscuit were inadequate, it struck him, as he carried them with care toward the large presence of Mrs. Cotton; but was not this inadequacy, after all, of a piece with the delicious and conventional unreality of an affair like this? He noticed a brilliant purple feather conspicuously waving from the top of Mrs. Cotton's bonnet, and was glad that everything was so bright. How pleasant it was on a summer day, how pleasant and harmless to play brilliantly at life! And, he thought with a smile, did not old Aristotle himself place Magnificence high among the virtues?

But Maple Fetters still had his anxious eye-glass fixed on the garden entrance.

"Miss Lamb—has Miss Lamb come?" Craik heard voices murmuring about him.

"No, not yet, but she's coming. Just heard Maple Fetters telling some one."

"Long says he can't understand it. In her note she said—"

"So quiet, so different!"

"They say in London—"

"Oh, yes; and here everybody, Professors, Heads of Houses. It's too amusing—"

"Well, she says she wants to study all the types."

"Ah, look, there she comes!"

Craik turned with the others, and saw Miss Lamb coming in through the Gothic archway. Her face was shaded with a large white hat, and her white dress, falling in long plain lines to her feet, brightened with the sun as she walked over the grass, out of the shadow of the building.

Long and Maple Fetters started forward, and escorted Miss Lamb and her aunt across

# Idyll

the lawn. They drew near to Craik and Mrs. Cotton.

"Oh, there is Mrs. Cotton," Miss Lamb exclaimed, and turned towards them. "Dear Mrs. Cotton," she said, "I was so hoping I should see you here!"

Craik looked at Miss Lamb. She rested her eyes on him for a second, then pressing Mrs. Cotton's hand, she stooped down with a graceful impulse and kissed the fat old thing. Craik overheard Mrs. Lyon, the wife of the president of All Saints, talking to the Warden of St. Simon's.

"Dear Miss Lamb!" she said in a deep and sentimental voice; "she is just as nice to women as she is to men."

"She is much nicer, surely," the ancient Warden replied with a cackling laugh; "she never kissed me!"

Miss Lamb had disappeared. And Mrs.

Cotton was busy discussing with philanthropic friends the affairs of Oxford charities.

"These Oxford parties are so nice," she said to Craik, as she turned her benevolent spectacles away from him; "they save one writing such heaps of notes."

Again Craik walked about alone, smiling and conspicuous; and although he tried to think that he was enjoying himself, he really wished very much to be up in his tower again, up there in its pleasant green shade and solitude. That, after all, was his place, the only place he was fit for; and he had better stick to it, and stick to his books, and not cast again the gloom of his presence on the social enjoyment of other more fortunate people. For he could not talk agreeably, and laugh and be gay; and, even if he could, which of the ladies who swept so prettily past him on the grass would ever care to listen to him? Thus resignedly musing, he retreated into the near shade of a laburnum tree, and, ceasing to smile in his fixed and weary way, he watched through the flowering branches the shining colours and placid agitation of the garden party. All the men except himself were moving among the groups of ladies, weaving darker threads into the brilliant pattern. Young Cobbe he saw, the captain of the College boat club, walking with Miss Lamb, walking and talking pleasantly, and he sighed; for although he was Cobbe's tutor, and well versed in his stupidity, he could not help envying the easy manners of the undergraduate.

But the half-real picture ceased to be a mere picture to him, and the sequence of images grew almost too vivid, when he noticed that Miss Lamb and her companion were coming directly to his tree. Could he manage to slip away without being seen? She was coming probably to pick a spray of the yellow flower to put in her white dress, or carry away perhaps as a memory of the party. And if he were found standing there like a policeman, it would be so awkward.

Miss Lamb fortunately met Maple Fetters, and, stopping herself, seemed to be sending him on to the tree alone. When he reached it, he pushed aside the branches and said, with a smile, "I say, Craik, I want to introduce you to Miss Lamb."

"Me?"

"Yes, you. We saw you here; she wants to meet you."

"Wants to meet *me*?"

"Yes, *you*. Come along."

Craik came out from beneath the tree.

"Miss Lamb—does she live in Oxford?"

"You don't mean to tell me you've never heard of Miss Lamb?" Fetters paused in astonishment. "You must be the only man in Oxford then who has not. Miss Lamb is an American!"

"An American?" Craik had heard that American ladies were so brilliant.

"Miss Lamb, let me introduce Mr. Craik, our philosopher."

"Mr. Craik, I am glad to meet you."

Craik bowed; then he saw that Miss Lamb had put out her hand; he tried to take it, but was too late. The American young lady however smiled, and put out her hand again, and gave it to him frankly, almost as if it were a present.

"We ought to shake hands, oughtn't we? It's the English way, isn't it?"

Craik stifled a guffaw, and his awkward sensations began to go.

"Mr. Cobbe, would you mind getting me an ice?"

Cobbe's face wore an odd expression as he bowed and disappeared. Maple Fetters fluttered off to other occupations. Craik and Miss Lamb were left alone, and they began to walk with vague steps, and, on the lady's part, vague, unfinished scraps of conversation, through the sunshine along the garden path. Then stopping, and resting her hands on her parasol, she said, as if they were old friends already, "I wonder—would you take me into your old College cloisters? I have heard so much about them, and it wouldn't be wrong for us to run away from the party for just a few minutes? I should so love to! You won't mind?"

"Oh dear, no!" Craik exclaimed. "Certainly we can go. It's through the quadrangle. But Mr. Cobbe, will he find you?"

"Oh, he'll know where I am; and if he doesn't it's no matter. Come!"

They went under the garden tower, and through the little old quadrangle, into the entrance of the cloisters. Of the history and traditions of the place, and of the whole College, Craik spoke almost with eloquence, while Miss Lamb listened with murmurs and interruptions of enthusiastic interest. The cloisters, as he explained, were once the cloisters of a monastery; the tower was the monastery tower; and the bell that hung there, and twice a day rang the College into chapel, was the bell that once sounded for the matins and vespers of the monks.

"What! monks? Did monks really once live here? Oh, how I should have liked to have seen it then!"

"Ah, but you couldn't, you know. They never allowed ladies inside the gates."

"How silly!"

"Yes," Craik said, smiling, "wasn't it silly?"

They walked with slow steps around the shadowed cloisters, and Miss Lamb talked idly of the party. It was such a pretty party, so amusing. Did he often go to garden parties? No! How odd! She did—to ever so many, in America, in London, and now in Oxford. The Oxford parties were the best though. Then suddenly she cried in a changed voice, "But how frivolous I am, Mr. Craik! I can see that you are quite shocked."

"Shocked! oh no, not at all."

"Well, then, you ought to be! Imagine being so frivolous in a solemn place like this. Tell me, you study philosophy, don't you? It must be splendid; I do envy you so! When I am in a place like Oxford I feel so frivolous, somehow, and ignorant. Why, I feel afraid—" Then after a moment's charming hesitation, "Yes, quite afraid to talk to clever people. You mustn't mind what I say, will you?"

"But I'm not clever!" he exclaimed. "Why—"

"Oh, but Mr. Craik! Why, you've written a book!"

"But that's nothing. And it's only a sort of study, nothing really."

"I wish I could read it."

"Oh no! don't try; it's a stupid thing, only meant for students."

Miss Lamb paused, and, turning her eyes to Craik with a look full of reproach, she said: "Ah! you are like the others, you don't think I am serious; you think I would not understand it!"

"Oh no, not that!" Craik urged in quick distress. "You would understand it, of course, what there is to understand. I only meant," he stammered, "I only meant that it was not well written, not interesting—not really worth reading, I mean."

"Oh, I'm sure it is worth reading, and I hear it's so clever. It is about Asia Minor, isn't it. Asia Minor is so interesting; I wish you would tell me something about it, and about your work. Do you like it here? Of course you do. Have you been in Oxford long?"

For a third time they passed round the cloister square, loitering with slow footsteps, through the old arches and past the epitaphs of the ancient celibate Fellows, and Craik, talking with an unreserve that was intimate and sudden, and yet somehow seemed quite natural to him, told about his work, and the writing of his book. Then, in answer to a question of Miss Lamb's, he described his quiet bringing up in an obsolete old town where his parents were tradespeople; his early schooling, how he had come to Oxford on a scholarship, and how he had stayed there ever since, living in the same College, his parents having died, and the Logic tutorship being offered to him just when he had taken his degree. So he seemed to have lived a long while there, in that sleepy old College, within its high walls and buildings: as an undergraduate first, busy and almost solitary, save for a few friends similar to himself; then as a tutor, still more busy with his work, and still more solitary; and above all, during the last few years, when all his thought and leisure had been given to his book on Ionic philosophers. How many years was it altogether? Eight; no, ten. And then, as she seemed to be really interested, he gave a sketch, half humorous and half serious, of his life in College, his amusements, his walks with Ranken. A bare, monastic life it seemed to himself when he came to describe it. So little to tell of in so many years; and how long ago it seemed!

"But dear me!" Craik exclaimed at last, with a blush, "I don't think I have ever talked so much of myself before. It sounds rather dull, I'm afraid."

Miss Lamb stopped for a moment.

"Dull, Mr. Craik," she cried, "oh no, I think it is noble! To have achieved so much already. You don't know how I have been interested! Only it is so—I mean it makes me seem so— so—. I suppose you hate women."

"Oh no—*no*!"

"I mean look down on them, despise them."

"No! why I—"

"I'm afraid you really do, only you're too polite to say so. You don't think, do you, that they could understand philosophy?"

# Idyll

"Of course they could, quite as well as we do, if they would only try."

"Do you think it would be any use my trying? Really, do you really? I should so love to, if it would be of any use. You know, I have always wanted to understand about it, and there is hardly anyone in the world I admire so much as the philosophers. They are the real leaders of the world—Socrates, and Emerson, and Herbert Spencer. And a frivolous life like mine seems sometimes so—; But then people will never believe I am in earnest, and they all make fun of me and discourage me so. Perhaps they are right; but I have never had any one to help me."

"Oh, I am sure they are wrong!" Craik cried. "If you would only try. Do you think I could—could help you?"

"Oh, you are too kind! And perhaps, if you wouldn't mind coming to see me some afternoon to talk to me about it. And maybe you would bring your book; I should so love to see it! And then if you would let me look at one or two of your lectures, those you have for just the stupidest of your pupils. No! don't tell me I'm not stupid, for I am, I assure you. And I have no right to ask you to come; you are so busy."

"Oh, but I should be only too delighted! If I may; if you don't think I should be a —with ladies, you know, I am always so afraid of being a bore."

She smiled at him.

"Ah, you do yourself injustice, Mr. Craik. Indeed you do! But come," she added suddenly, "we must be going back to the garden. How I hate to leave this dear old cloister!"

"Must we really go?"

"Yes, we really must. Isn't it horrid, when

you have had such an interesting talk, to have to go back and say stupid and silly things to stupid and silly people?"

They left the cloisters and, crossing the quadrangle, they stopped for a moment, and looked at the blue picture set in an archway of grey walls, the blue picture of the afternoon light and air in the depth and distance of the garden.

"How pretty! It's like,—what is it like?"

"Like standing in the past, and looking into the present?" Craik romantically suggested.

"Yes, it's like that. But I mean the people, the way they look so far off and blue, as if they were under water. There's something else it reminds me of."

"A tank at an aquarium, when you look through the plate glass?"

"Yes, it *is* like that, really!"

"With Professors and Heads of Houses swimming about like old fat carp."

"Oh, Mr. Craik, how can you? For shame!"

She paused again when she got through the archway.

"Tell me, Mr. Craik," she said, "is this the tower you live in? And the gargoyle you told me about? I should so like to see him. He must be charming. That face up there, peering over the roof? Oh yes, I see. How too delightful! My! isn't that quaint? Just think, he looks back on the past, and on the present, and on the town; and it symbolizes—symbolizes—Life, doesn't it?"

"Yes,—perhaps it does," Craik said rather dubiously.

"He hasn't exactly a kind expression," said Miss Lamb, looking up again.

## Idyll

"No," Craik answered, looking up himself and laughing. "That's his way. Then to-day he's shocked at seeing so many ladies here. He doesn't like ladies, you know."

"How horrid of him! Why, what harm can we do here?"

"Harm! Why, Miss Lamb," Craik said with quaint politeness, "your visits are our greatest blessings!"

Craik knew the old garden well, he thought, and he had certainly been in it in all weathers. But to-day it came over him that he had never seen the place before looking so oddly green and shining. Certainly, when he and Ranken had walked there—poor Ranken! Craik smiled a little.

"What are you smiling at?" Miss Lamb asked.

"Smiling?" Craik said in embarrassment. "Why, was I smiling?"

"Certainly you were. It is strange, really it is, how much you are like a friend of mine in America. The way you smile reminds me so much of him. Really it is quite funny, the resemblance. But perhaps you don't like to be told you look like other people?"

"Oh yes, I do." Then he added, after a pause, with desperate and awkward courage, "if they are friends of yours."

Miss Lamb did not seem to notice either his compliment or his blush.

"How odd you should know Mr. Ranken," she said musingly. "I've not seen him lately. Is he as sentimental as ever?"

"Ranken of St. Thomas'! Why, he's not sentimental. It must be someone else."

"He used to be then; I'm sure it is Mr. Ranken of St. Thomas'. I met him last summer at Dieppe. We went on picnics. But, Mr. Craik," she added, laughing, "really this garden is like Paradise! The undergraduates must fancy they have got back into the Garden of Eden."

"Indeed you would think so," said Craik, "from the way they avoid the tree of knowledge! They are so much cleverer than Adam."

They were in the midst of the party now, and Craik was proud, though somewhat embarrassed, with the attention they attracted, and Mrs. Cotton's smiles of obvious encouragement. Indeed he was almost glad when Cobbe joined them and, planting himself in front of Miss Lamb, exclaimed, "Well, Miss Lamb, well! Here I've been waiting half-an-hour with this ice, it's melted into soup."

"I'm so sorry," Miss Lamb cried. "Come, let's get another." Then she turned her eyes to Craik and said, giving him her hand in her friendly manner, "Good-bye, Mr. Craik, good-bye; you won't forget? To-morrow, isn't it?"

### III.

Craik took off his hat; wiped his forehead; tried to get rid of some of the dust on his boots, and then he rang the bell.

"Is Miss Lamb at home?"

"Yes, sir; Miss Lamb is in the garden."

Entering, Craik saw a number of hats and sticks in the hall. Miss Lamb, he thought, must have several brothers. He put down his stick, and the book with it, after a moment's hesitation; that was better, he would leave it there and would come and fetch it when the conversation turned that way. Then, buttoning up his black coat over the lecture notes that filled his pocket, he followed the servant through the house out into the little garden. It was full of strong sunlight, and there were several undergraduates there. One was up in a tree;

# Idyll

Cobbe lay in a hammock smoking, and another of Craik's pupils lay on the grass at Miss Lamb's feet, rolling lemons. He stopped for a moment.

"Oh Mr. Corn—Mr. Craik, I mean," Miss Lamb called out in a friendly voice, "I am so glad to see you."

Craik advanced with an awkward smile, and Miss Lamb reached out her right hand most cordially. In her left hand she held a lemon-squeezer.

"How good of you to come! And isn't it hot? Exactly like America, I've been saying. We've just come out into the garden without our hats. Won't you sit down on that rug, if you don't mind? Oh, I nearly forgot; let me introduce you to my aunt, Mrs. Stacey. I guess you know everybody else."

Craik shook hands with a lady who was sitting and knitting in an arbour, nodded to the undergraduates, and then settled down on a rug in the sunshine. How he wished that he had not decided at the last moment to wear a tall hat and a long coat! The undergraduates were all in flannels.

Miss Lamb spoke of the garden party.

"Your lovely college! It is *too* ideal; it is like a dream. And the cloisters too! You don't know how solemn it made me feel. Now, you needn't laugh, Mr. Cobbe, I really did feel solemn—more solemn, I guess, than you have ever been. Gracious, it *is* hot!" she added, with a sudden change of subject. "Mr. Craik, let me give you some of this lemon squash; I made it myself."

"Thanks! I shall be most pleased to have some." Craik's voice seemed to himself to be formal, and his phrase pedantic.

"Oh, but what was I saying?" Miss Lamb went on, looking at the company generally.

"You were telling us how solemn you were," Cobbe suggested. "Wasn't it rather a new experience?"

"Now, Mr. Cobbe, what a horrid thing to say," she replied, with great good-nature. "You're his tutor, Mr. Craik, aren't you? Well, next time you have a chance, I hope you'll set him some real horrid work to do. I'm sure he needs it."

Miss Lamb said this casually, with a pleasant laugh, as she fanned herself. No one answered; Craik, and even Cobbe coloured, and the undergraduate in the tree suppressed a titter.

But Mrs. Stacey at this moment asked by happy chance some question of Craik, addressing him as "Professor Craik," in her high American voice, and he hastened to answer her with effusion.

"Oh, I say," one of the undergraduates

exclaimed, "that was a splendid score of yours, Miss Lamb, off the Warden. Perhaps you've not heard it, Mr. Craik, the joke about the Garden of Eden?" he said, turning to Craik, who had come to an end of his conversation with Mrs. Stacey. "The Warden was showing Miss Lamb the garden, when she said to him, 'Why it is like the Garden of Eden here, Mr. Warden; only I suppose you are wiser than Adam, and don't disturb the Tree of Knowledge.'"

"My dear," Mrs. Stacey cried, "you didn't really speak so to the sweet old Warden?"

"But, I say," Cobbe exclaimed, "how's this, Miss Lamb? Long and Maple Fetters tell that story as having been got off them, and they seemed to think that they rather scored off you."

"They didn't a bit; they were only silly!"

"Then you did get it off on them?"

# Idyll

"No, I didn't."

"Oh, now, that explains," another undergraduate interposed, "that explains the story Mrs. Cotton was trying to tell. It seemed, as she told it, to have no point at all. 'Mr. Warden,' she made you say, 'Mr. Warden, you have a lovely garden here, but I am told you never pick the fruit.' 'The Warden, you know, is so particular about his figs,' Mrs. Cotton added, 'it is quite a joke with all the Fellows.'"

Miss Lamb was silent. After a little while, however, when a few other anecdotes of Mrs. Cotton had been told, and they came to the well-known story of that lady and the cow in St. Giles's, she began to smile, and before long was quite consumed with merriment, for a siphon of soda-water, fizzing off by mistake in the hands of one of the undergraduates, had sprinkled itself over Cobbe.

"You did that on purpose, Galpin, I know you did," he cried, jumping out of the hammock and shaking himself.

"Oh, no, he didn't!" Miss Lamb said, shaking with laughter. "Indeed, I'm sure he wouldn't for worlds!"

Her attention was then taken by the youth up in the tree, who had been throwing down leaves and bits of sticks on the heads of the party below. A piece of bark falling into the jug of lemon squash, Miss Lamb feigned great wrath and indignation.

"I wanted to give Mr. Craik some more; but oh, you haven't drunk what you have! Isn't it sweet enough for you?"

"It is just right, thank you," he said, and he took up the glass, tepid now from standing in the sun, and was just going to drink it, when the young lady cried: "Oh, wait a moment, please; there's a poor little insect tumbled into it. Dear little thing! Do take it out—oh, be careful! I can't bear to see anything suffer."

Craik fished the insect out of the lemonade with a blade of grass, and Miss Lamb, putting it down on the ground, poked it tenderly in aid of its moist attempts to crawl away. Ultimately Craik rose from his uncomfortable posture on the ground. It was a long while, it seemed to him, that he had been sitting there, smiling and solemn in the sunshine, and casting about in his mind for an excuse to go; while the others he envied so—the youth perched up in the tree, Miss Lamb fanning herself and squeezing lemons, Cobbe smoking and slowly swinging in the hammock, laughed and lazily talked, as if their life was one afternoon of endless Arcadian leisure. But Craik had a morbid sense that his shadow, which he glanced at now and then, had been growing, almost as if he were swelling, he and his top hat, and casting a larger shade on the little garden.

"Well, I must be going! We college tutors, you know," he said, feeling pretty stiff in body and mind, but attempting nevertheless a little jauntiness of air.

"Oh, but, Mr. Craik, you mustn't go now!" Miss Lamb cried, "really you mustn't. Why, we're all going up the river to have late tea at Godstow, and come home by moonlight; and I'm going to take my banjo. I hoped you would come with us!"

"I'm sorry, but I must be back."

"Well, I'm really sorry, too; I am, indeed. You must come again." She held his hand in hers for a second, and there was something appealing in her manner. "Now you will come again, won't you? It's—it's rather hot just to-day for philosophy, isn't it?" she added, her face brightening with a friendly and apologetic smile.

Craik found his hat and stick, but not his book, in the hall.

"I've left a book here," he said to the maid.

"Oh, I beg your pardon, sir, I thought it was for Miss Lamb, so I put it on the shelf where she puts the other university gentlemen's books that they sends. I'll go and bring it, sir."

"Is this it?" she called from a neighbouring room—"'Elements of Pishcology?'"

"No," said Craik, hurriedly; "it's about Asia Minor. 'Life and Thought in—'"

"'In Hearly Asia Minor,' sir?"

"Yes, that's mine," Craik answered, in a voice that was not without a touch of melancholy.

*Buller Intervening*

# Buller Intervening

As Vaughan was walking towards the underground station one of those bleak mornings last winter, he saw, coming the same way, a man who had been at College in his time—one Buller by name; and Buller, when he caught sight of Vaughan, began to smile, but when they met, he exclaimed, in a mock mournful voice, "I say, have you heard about poor Crabbe?"

"You mean his political speech, when his spectacles were smashed, and he had to take to the woods?" asked Vaughan, beating his hands and stamping, for the cold was bitter.

"Oh no, that's ancient. I mean"—and Buller's voice broke with laughter—"I mean his engagement!"

"Crabbe! oh, nonsense!"

"Gospel fact, I'll take my oath on it. Fancy Crabbe!" and again his laughter froze into white puffs of breath about his head. They went into the station together, and bought their tickets. Crabbe engaged! Vaughan tried to picture him as an accepted lover. Poor Crabbe! They had all hoped that his Fellowship and his work on the metres of Catullus would keep him out of mischief. But they might have known—those prize fellows, with so much time on their hands; and Crabbe above all, with his fixed idea that he was cut out for a man of action!

"But tell me about Crabbe," Vaughan said,

## Buller Intervening

as they waited on the platform; "have you seen him?"

"Oh yes. The other day I ran up to have a look at the 'Torpid.' It's all right now."

"The Torpid?"

"No; I mean about Crabbe."

"You think it's a good match, then?"

"Good match! No, I mean that I went and talked to him myself."

"And he was engaged?"

"He *was*," said Buller, laughing; "poor old beast!" The train drew in, and when they had taken their seats, Buller leaned over, and, with a low voice, went on telling his story in Vaughan's ear. "You see, I went up to Oxford, and down at the barge Blunt tells me about old Crabbe; and when I go into College the first person I meet is the Dean, looking as chirpy as ever. How those old parsons do keep it up!

"'Well, sir,' says I, 'and what do you think of Crabbe's engagement?'

"'Perfect rot,' says the Dean. 'The girl had no money; how were they going to live? Crabbe would have to chuck his Catullus—everything.'

"'How did it happen?' I asked. 'Crabbe never used to be sweet on the ladies.' 'No; but in reading Catullus, Crabbe had got some ideas,' the Dean said, with a kind of wink."

Here Vaughan could not help interrupting the story. "Come, Buller," he whispered, "it must have been Blunt who said that. The old Dean couldn't talk in that way."

But Buller felt sure it was the Dean. "You see, you don't know the old boy; he's quite another person with me. Anyhow, that's the way Crabbe got into it. And he went on, the Dean said, to read all sorts of other poetry, especially that man—what you may call him? They had a society—"

" Browning ? "

"Yes, that's the man. Well, Crabbe thought it all very fine and exciting, the Dean said; he used to read them Browning in the Common Room, and there was one thing he seemed specially taken with—Browning's theory of love."

"What was that?" Vaughan asked, for it was a joy to hear Buller talking of literature.

"Well," Buller whispered, "you see this man Browning hates all your shilly-shallying about; he thinks that when you fall in love, you ought to go your whole pile, even if you come a cropper after. It's all rot, of course, the Dean said; but poor Crabbe thought it was real, and went and proposed to a young woman he had met once or twice.

So there he was, engaged! And he seemed to think himself the hell of a duke, the Dean said; but everyone else in Oxford thought he was making a bl—"

"Oh, Buller," Vaughan interposed, "really, you mustn't put such words into the Dean's mouth!"

"Well, I don't quite remember the old boy's lingo, but, at any rate, the Dean thought Crabbe was making a fool of himself. 'I think I can settle it,' says I to the Dean. 'I wish you would,' said the Dean; so off I go to Crabbe's rooms. He came in just as I got there; I wish you could have seen him—a frock-coat, top-hat, flower in his button-hole, his hair plastered down. And only last year, it was, that he got up as a Socialist, with a red silk handkerchief in his hat! But now he shook hands with me up in the air; was most affable and condescending; assured me he was glad to see his old pals—especially friends from London. Oxford people were very well in their way, but narrow, and rather donnish. Didn't I notice it in coming from London?

"Well, this was almost too much from Crabbe, but I thought it would be more sport to draw him out a bit. So we got to talking; I didn't let on I knew he was engaged, but after a bit I began to talk about marriage and love and all that in a general sort of way. Old Crabbe swallows it all, talks a lot of literary stuff. 'Fall in love, Buller,' says he, 'fall in love, and live! Let me read you what thing-a-majig says,' and he gets down a book —who did you say he was? Browning, yes, that's the man—he gets down a book of Browning's and begins to read—you ought to have seen him, his face got pink; and at the end he says, with a proud smile, as if the poem was all about him, 'Isn't that ripping,

Buller, isn't that brave, isn't that the way to take life!'

"'Do you mind if I smoke?' said I.

"'Smoke? Oh, do certainly,' and Crabbe sits down looking rather foolish. But after a moment, he says in an easy sort of way, 'Ah, I meant to ask you about all the chaps in London—getting on all right? any of them married?'

"'Married!' says I, 'O Lord, no; *they* don't want to dish themselves.'

"'Dish themselves,' says Crabbe, 'why, what do you mean?'

"'I mean what I say; if you get married without any money, you're dished, that's all—I mean practical people, who want to get on.'

"Then Crabbe began to talk big; one shouldn't care only for success—it might be practical, perhaps, but he did not mean to sacrifice the greatest thing in life for money.

"'The greatest thing in life—what's that?'"

Buller laughed so loudly at this part of his story, that the other people in the carriage began to stare at him and Vaughan. So he went on in a lower whisper. "'What's that?' says I.

"'I mean,' says Crabbe, 'why, what I have been talking about.'

"'Well, what is it?'

"'What I was saying a little while ago.'

"'But you talked too fast—I couldn't catch it; give us the tip, out with it.'

"'I mean love, passion,' says he.

"'What? say it again.'

"'Well, I mean—and it's always said that love—the poets—'

"'The who?'

"'The poets.'" Again Buller laughed out loud.

"'Oh, poets!' says I, 'I thought you said

porters. Poets! so you've been reading poets, have you? but you oughtn't to believe all that—why, they don't mean it themselves; they write it because they're expected to, but it's all faked up—I know how it's done.'

"Old Crabbe begins to talk in his big way. I let him go on for a while, but then I said, 'See here, Crabbe, it's all very well to read that literary stuff, and I suppose it's what you're paid for doing. But don't go and think it's all true, because it isn't, and the sooner you know it the better.' 'There was a man I knew once,' says I, 'who got fearfully let in by just this sort of thing; Oxford don too, Fellow of Queen's named Peake; took to reading poetry; he went to Brighton in the Long, with his head full of it all. Wild sea waves, the moon and all the rest of it; and back comes Peake married; had to turn out of his College rooms, went to live at the other end of nowhere, stuffy little house, full of babies, had to work like a nigger, beastly work too; coached me for Smalls, that's how I know him; no time for moon and sea waves now; and it all came from reading poetry.'

"Old Crabbe begins to sit up at this. 'But I don't see,' he says, 'I don't see why—didn't he have his Fellowship money?'

"'But you don't suppose that's going to support a wife and a lot of children.'

"'Oh, if he had children,' says Crabbe, and the old boy begins to blush and says, 'I don't see the need.'

"'Much you know about it, Crabbe,' says I, and I couldn't help laughing, he looked such an idiot.

"'Well, anyhow,' he says, 'your friend may have been unfortunate, but I respect him all the same; he was bold, he lived.'

"'What does all that mean?—he didn't die, of course!'

"'I mean he loved—he had that.'

"'Oh yes, he had, but I rather think he wished he hadn't. He said it didn't come to much—and even when he was engaged she used to bore him sometimes.'

"'Really!' says old Crabbe, 'that's odd now,' and then he goes on, as if he was talking to himself, 'I wonder if everyone feels like that?'

"'Of course they do! But after you're married, just think of it—never quiet, never alone; Peake said it nearly drove him wild. And to think he was tied up like that for the rest of his life!'

"'Yes, it is a long time.' Crabbe began to look rather green. 'Your friend—his name was Peake, I think you said—I suppose he couldn't have broken off the engagement?' and he smiled in a sort of sea-sick way.

"'Of course he could,' says I, as I got up to go. 'Perfect ass not to—but good-bye, Crabbe, you've got jolly rooms here.'

"'Yes, they are nice,' says Crabbe in a kind of sinking voice.

"So, a day or two after, I meet the Dean; the old boy seems very much pleased. 'Well Buller, I think you've done the biz,' says he; 'I don't believe old Crabbe will do it after all.'"

When he had finished his story, Buller leaned comfortably back. "I felt sure he would get out of it somehow," he said aloud, "I think that story finished him." "You know what I mean," he added, nodding significantly, "that story of Peake."

"I don't believe Peake ever existed!" Vaughan answered, as low as he could.

Buller leaned forward again, he was almost bursting with laughter. "Of course he didn't!" he hissed in Vaughan's ear. "But wasn't Crabbe in a blue funk though!"

"Oh, I don't believe Crabbe minded you a bit. I'm sure he won't break it off," Vaughan whispered indignantly. "And what right had you to talk that way? I never heard of such impertinent meddling!"

"Bet you three to one he does," Buller whispered back. "Come, man, make it a bet!" The train drew into the Temple station and Vaughan got up.

"I won't bet on anything of the kind," he said, as he stood at the door. "And what do you know about love anyhow, Buller? Then think of the poor girl, she probably believes that Crabbe is a hero, a god—"

"Well, she won't for long," Buller chuckled.

*The Optimist*

# The Optimist

WHAT was he doing there? why didn't he ride on? Mrs. Ross wondered, as she watched with some astonishment the tall young man who was staring in at the gate. But in a moment her husband left the hedge he was trimming, and waved his shears at the stranger, who thereupon came in, pushing his bicycle with him along the drive. When the two young men met, they seemed to greet each other like old acquaintances. Probably he was one of George's Oxford friends, she thought, beginning to feel a little shy, as they walked towards her across the grass. The bicyclist was thin and very tall; his shadow, in the late sunshine, seemed to stretch endlessly over the grass. His face was bathed in perspiration; he was grey with dust, and altogether he looked very shabby by the side of her good-looking husband.

"Mary, I want to introduce my friend, Mr. Allen, to you." Mrs. Ross was always a little afraid of her husband's friends; then Allen was a don at Oxford, and she knew he was considered extremely clever. However she greeted him in her friendly, charming way. He would have tea, of course?

Allen gripped her hand, smiling awkwardly. No, he wouldn't have tea, and he was afraid it was very late for calling; he must apologize; indeed, when he got to the gate, he had hesitated about coming in.

Oh, no! it wasn't late, she assured him;

and her husband declared he must stay to dinner. He had never seen the Grange before and, of course, they must show him everything.

"Oh, I don't think I can stay to dinner," Allen murmured, looking through his spectacles at his dusty clothes. But at last he consented though doubtfully; he was staying at Sunbridge, he explained, and it was rather a long ride over.

Ross took him to the house; soon he reappeared, well brushed, his pale and thoughtful face pink with scrubbing. They walked with him about the gardens, then they went to their little farm, showing him the cows and horses, and the new-built hayrick.

George Ross was a young land agent who, not long after leaving Oxford, had had the luck to get a good appointment; and for more than a year he and his young wife had been living here in the most absurdly happy way. Now and then his Oxford friends would come to visit him, and it filled Ross with delight and pride to show them over his new domain.

As they came back from the farm through the garden, Ross stopped a moment. "Doesn't the house look well from here!" he said to Allen. The roofs, gables, and trees stood out dark against the golden west; the garden, with its old red walls, sweet peas, and roses, was filled with mellow light.

Allen gazed at the view through his spectacles, and expressed a proper admiration. But of himself he seemed to notice nothing, and Mrs. Ross was rather hurt by the way he went past her borders of flowers without ever looking at them.

"You see it's just the kind of life that suits me—suits both of us," Ross explained;

"I don't see how I could have found anything better. Of course," he added modestly, "of course some men might not think much of work like this. But I consider myself tremendously fortunate—I didn't really deserve such luck."

"Quite so," Allen assented in a way that Mrs. Ross thought rather odd, till she decided that it was merely absent-mindedness. Every now and then she would look at Allen—the tall, thin, threadbare young man puzzled her a little; he seemed so extremely dull and embarrassed; and yet there was a thoughtful, kind look in his eyes that she liked. And anyhow he was George's friend; so, as they walked rather silently and awkwardly about, waiting for dinner, she tried to talk to him, making remarks in her eager way, and glancing sometimes at her husband for fear he might be laughing at her. Such subjects as bicycling, the roads, the weather, and life in Oxford, were started, and they both talked to their guest with the exaggerated politeness of newly married people, who would much rather be talking to each other. Yes, the road over was very pretty, Allen agreed. But was there a river? He remembered noticing how pretty the road was, but he had not noticed that it ran by any river. And all their questions he answered with a certain eagerness, but in a way that somehow made the subject drop.

"Well, I finished the hedge," Ross said at last, turning to his wife. "You said I wouldn't."

"Oh, but wait till I see it for myself!"

The young man looked at her gloomily. "You see how it is, Allen, she doesn't believe her husband's word!"

"Oh, hush, George," she said, and they both began to laugh like children. Then they turned to Allen again. Was he comfortable where he was staying? she asked.

Well no, honestly, it wasn't very comfortable, Allen replied. To tell the truth, he was rather disappointed in the place. He had gone there after hearing some undergraduates describe it, and tell how amusing they had found the people. But, somehow, he had not found the people different from people anywhere else. But then he had only made the acquaintance of one man—

"Well, didn't he turn out to be an old poacher, or a gipsy, or something romantic?" asked Mrs. Ross.

"No, not at all—he was a Methodist Calvinist deacon, who gave me a lift one wet afternoon, and lectured me all the way about Temperance. And, of course," Allen added, with rather a comic smile, "and, of course, I was already a total abstainer." They all laughed at this.

What was he working at over there? Ross asked him a few minutes afterwards. He was writing a paper, Allen replied; but what it was about Mrs. Ross did not understand. She hoped her husband would ask something more, but he merely said, "I see," without much interest, adding that he had not read any philosophy for years.

When they sat down to dinner, the lady's evening dress, the silver and flowers on the table, seemed to make Allen all the more awkward and conscious of his appearance. However, he plainly meant to do his best to talk, and, after a moment's silence, he remarked that he supposed the theory of farming was very interesting.

"Yes, it is," said Mrs. Ross, "and it's such fun ploughing in the autumn, and in the spring seeing the young green things come up."

"I suppose the climate is a great factor in the problem."

"Oh, of course, everything depends on that; suppose it comes on to rain just when you've cut your hay!"

Ross began to laugh. "I believe my wife thinks of nothing but hay now."

"You farm yourself, don't you?" Allen asked, looking at her rather timidly.

"Oh, a little; I always say I manage our little farm, and I'm going to learn to plough. And I keep chickens—this is one of mine—poor little thing!" she added.

"She pretends to be sorry now, but when she has a chance to sell her chickens I never saw anyone so bloodthirsty."

"Oh, George, how can you say such things? Don't believe him, Mr. Allen. And anyhow," she added (it seemed a platitude, but platitudes were better than absolute silence), "anyhow, I suppose it is what the chickens are meant for."

To her surprise this mild remark led to an animated argument. For Allen, in agreeing with her, said something about "the general scheme of things." Ross began to laugh at this, and asked Allen if he still held to that old system of his. Allen answered this question so earnestly, that the lady looked at him with wonder.

Yes! he held to it more firmly than ever; he was sure it could be maintained! Indeed, seriously he had come to feel more and more that you must accept something of the kind. Ross dissented in a joking way, but Allen would not be put off; he began talking rapidly and eagerly, almost forgetting his dinner as he argued. He drank a great deal of cold water, and his thin face grew quite flushed with excitement.

## The Optimist

Mrs. Ross looked from one to the other with puzzled eyes; probably that was the way they had been used to talk at Oxford, but what it was about she could not understand. She only felt sorry for Allen, he evidently cared so much, was as anxious to prove his point as if his whole life depended on it, while her husband seemed to treat the whole thing rather as a joke.

Soon she gave up trying to listen, and though the sound of their voices was in her ears, her mind wandered out into the garden, to the farm and meadows. But Allen's voice, appealing to her, called her suddenly back. "I'm sure you agree with me, Mrs. Ross," he said, without the least shyness. He plainly looked on her now as nothing but a mind which might agree or disagree. "I'm sure you must regard it as existing for rational ends."

"But what do you mean by 'It,' Mr. Allen?" she asked, very much puzzled.

"Why, the universe, of course."

"Oh, I don't know," she said, shaking her head and laughing. "It makes me dizzy to think of it. As for George, I wouldn't mind what he says, Mr. Allen; he believes all sorts of dreadful things, and he's always making fun—look how he's laughing at me now. George, will you have your coffee in here, or in the drawing-room?"

"Oh, in the drawing-room—we'll come in a minute, when we've settled the universe."

As she went out, she heard them still arguing.

And they had not ended it when they came into the drawing-room a little later.

"But I deny that pain is an evil. I appeal to you," Allen said, turning to Mrs. Ross; "don't you think that pain is necessary?"

"But necessary for what, Mr. Allen?"

"Why, if we want to be really happy, I mean," he went on, trying to make himself quite clear, "I mean, suppose we lived as they do in the Tropics, sitting under trees all day."

Ross also turned to her, "Well, Mary, tell us what you think?"

Mrs. Ross laughed. "I'm afraid I'm not a fair judge, Mr. Allen, I'm so fond of sitting under trees, and I must say I think it sounds rather nice. Do you have sugar in your coffee?"

"No sugar, thanks. But surely," he went on as if he had an argument now that would be certain to convince a lady. "Surely a certain amount of discomfort is an advantage! Now, take a child for instance, to educate it you have to make it suffer."

"Oh, indeed you don't, Mr. Allen," she said so promptly, and in such a voice, that Allen seemed a little disconcerted.

## The Optimist

Ross begged for a little music. She sat down to the piano and began to play—with a little emotion at first, which soon died out of the quiet sounds. The window was open on the lawn; the faint light, the odours of the garden, mingled with the soft music.

They sat in silence for a moment. At last Allen rose; he must be going, he said, he had his paper to finish.

"But it is nice here," he added, with half a sigh, as if vaguely aware, for a moment, of the romantic happiness about him. Then his mind seemed to revert to the argument; if Ross would only read Hegel's *Logic*—

"Well, we might read it aloud in the evenings perhaps," the young man answered, laughing. "Have you got a lamp on your machine?" "Yes, I think there is." They went out to the gate and, lighting his lamp, they sent him off into the twilight. Then they walked slowly back towards the house. A few stars were kindled above the dim trees; the air was fragrant with the scent of the hay, and through the stillness the faint noise of life came across the meadows—a woman singing, the voices of children, and sleepy sounds of cattle.

"How good it is!" the young man said, drawing his companion closer to him. "But people are always coming, aren't they? It's dreadful! we never do seem to see anything of each other."

"No, do we! But he's a nice man, Mr. Allen. I liked him."

"Oh, old Allen's a good sort."

"What does he do—how does he live in Oxford?"

"He teaches philosophy, and lives on bread and tea in little lodgings."

"It sounds awfully dreary—"

## The Optimist

"Well, it is rather dreary for him, poor man. I wouldn't be there for a good deal."

"But, tell me, what was that he was arguing about?"

"Oh, that's his philosophy; he's always arguing about it. He believes in a kind of Hegelianism."

"What is that?"

"Oh, it's a view of things; he's what you call an Optimist."

"But I thought an Optimist was a person who was very happy?"

"No; it only means a man who believes that you ought to be happy, that you are meant to enjoy life—that the world is good."

"But you don't mean that he was trying to *prove* that?"

"Why, yes, you heard him; he's always at it when you give him a chance. He thinks it must be so, that you can deduce it from the first principles of things."

But Mrs. Ross could not be made to understand it. To her it seemed that either you were happy or you weren't. "And, then, fancy trying to prove it to us!" she kept saying.

At last she took her husband's arm to go in; but still stood for a moment in silence thinking it over. "That poor Mr. Allen!" she exclaimed at last, "an Optimist, you said he was?"

www.ingramcontent.com/pod-product-compliance
Lightning Source LLC
Chambersburg PA
CBHW032112230426
43672CB00009B/1715